Why Should We Study
The Constitution?

"The answer is simple enough . . . because this Constitution is the most important thing in the lives of every person living in the United States. Your way of life is built around it, your government is based upon it, and your rights and privileges as United States citizens are protected by it.

"To be ignorant of the Constitution is to be ignorant of all the things your country is . . . and of the truths its people have believed to be above all others in the relationships between human beings and government."

—*Floyd G. Cullop*

FLOYD G. CULLOP has 17 years of experience as a history teacher in junior and senior high schools in Monroe County, Tennessee.

The CONSTITUTION *of the* UNITED STATES:

An Introduction

By Floyd G. Cullop

UPDATED EDITION

A MENTOR BOOK

MENTOR
Published by the Penguin Group
Penguin Putnam Inc., 375 Hudson Street,
New York, New York 10014, U.S.A.
Penguin Books Ltd, 27 Wrights Lane,
London W8 5TZ, England
Penguin Books Australia Ltd, Ringwood,
Victoria, Australia
Penguin Books Canada Ltd, 10 Alcorn Avenue,
Toronto, Ontario, Canada M4V 3B2
Penguin Books (N.Z.) Ltd, 182–190 Wairau Road,
Auckland 10, New Zealand

Penguin Books Ltd, Registered Offices:
Harmondsworth, Middlesex, England

Published by Mentor, an imprint of Dutton NAL,
a member of Penguin Putnam Inc.

First Signet Printing, October, 1969
First Mentor Printing, May, 1984
32 31 30 29 28 27 26 25

 REGISTERED TRADEMARK—MARCA REGISTRADA

Printed in the United States of America

Preface to the Second Edition

July 4, 1976, marked the two-hundredth anniversary of the Declaration of Independence of the United States. It was a date anticipated by millions of published words; by production of innumerable souvenir collectibles; by television productions; and by local plans of celebration throughout the country. In fact, July 4 is celebrated as Independence Day each and every year, and ranks with Christmas and Easter as the most readily identifiable holidays our nation has.

Has anyone celebrated March 4? Not recently. Not in living memory. Yet March 4, 1789, is a date of equal importance to our nation as July 4, 1776.

A lasting victory was won on this date. A victory of intellect. A rare victory indeed. So rare some historians maintain it has been accomplished only three times during all of human history: Old Testament Israel, the Golden Age of Greece, and the era of emergence of the United States of America.

March 4, 1789, is the date the Constitution of the United States of America became the supreme law of the nation.

March 4, 1989, the two-hundredth anniversary of the Constitution, is close to us. Our form of government has been in existence for two centuries, making it, at present, the oldest continuous constitutional government based on a written constitution in the world.

Constitutional government has provided two important blessings: (1) It united the states as a single entity, setting the stage for strength and growth not possible under smaller semi-independent units, thus protecting us from tyranny abroad; and (2) It stated the rights of the individual and the limitations of government, thus protecting us from tyranny at home.

The Constitution is eloquent in its simplicity and precision of language, though the language to us today may seem somewhat archaic. It is also eloquent in what it does not say, for it is this which makes it flexible, amendable, durable, and open to judicial interpretation.

March 4 is an important anniversary. Let us celebrate in 1989 and thereafter.

The United States Constitution is often difficult to read and understand. Many times students dread having to begin the study of it in school. I know, because I have taught the information found in the Constitution to young people in grades eight to twelve.

The same question is always asked: "Why do we have to study this thing?" The answer is simple enough. This "thing"—this Constitution—is the most important thing in the life of every person living in the United States. Your way of life is built around it, your government is based upon it, and your rights and privileges as United States citizens are protected by it. To be ignorant of it is to be ignorant of all the things your country is, and of the truths its people have believed to be above all others in the relationships between human beings and government. In order to truly enjoy, appreciate, and protect what you have as citizens of the United States, you must be aware of what is found in your Constitution.

In the writing of this book, explanations have been kept simple—easy to read and understand without putting aside detail. Vocabulary taken from the original text of the Constitution, along with words and terms of explanation the reader might find unfamiliar, have been defined in parentheses immediately after they have been used. Study quizzes and lists of difficult words, with their definitions, are spaced throughout the book. The simplified text is followed by the Constitution in its original wording, and in the final section of the book, "Know Your Q's and A's," 203 questions about the Constitution have been answered.

This book has been written with two purposes in mind: (1) to explain our Constitution in terms that may be easily understood; and (2) to define the language of the original text so clearly that the student will then be able to read and comprehend the actual wording of the Constitution itself.

F.G.C.

CONTENTS

PART III:

THE BILL OF RIGHTS

your future brother-in-law. One ghost haunting
the carriage house is plenty.

She'd forgotten that he'd been meeting his future
brother-in-law—Richard Montague—that day. It
was one of a thousand insignificant exchanges she'd
had with Ike, and there'd been no reason to attach
any importance to where he'd gone that morning.
After all, he hadn't been *missing*.

But he was now, Tess thought. She just hadn't
realized it until the past few days.

Maybe he'd never made it to the carriage house.
Maybe he'd left town before his meeting there with
Richard Montague.

Tess checked ten more e-mails, refusing to let her
thoughts rush ahead, and as she read, she remembered the easy banter between Ike and herself. It
wasn't just on his end—it was on hers, too, but without the slashing wit, the thrill of poking at other
people's weaknesses.

Ike had loved Joanna Thorne, and he'd believed
Richard Montague, who was about to marry his sister, Lauren, was partly responsible for Joanna's mal-
aise. The woman had worked for him, and anyone
who worked for Richard Montague had to be as con-
sumed with getting him to Washington as he was.
She hadn't made all the connections until now, perhaps because she hadn't known the players, perhaps
because she'd been so occupied with sorting out her

own life and hadn't paid proper attention to what was going on with Ike.

The reference to Joanna working for Richard was in a note from Ike copied at the bottom of one of Tess's e-mails to him. She hadn't kept the original.

Whether he was a client or perhaps even a friend, her relationship with Ike, she now saw, had been a guilty pleasure. She hadn't really known the people he'd trashed with his cutting, often very funny wit. Now she felt like a coconspirator, although she couldn't bring herself to regret their relationship. He'd never meant people to take him seriously. He was an overgrown adolescent who believed everyone should forgive his excesses because he was a good guy at heart. Tess had never expected anything from him—Ike Grantham was what he was.

But, she thought, he really hadn't liked Richard Montague at all.

She sat back, her head pounding. "Susanna, yesterday Richard Montague told me he hadn't been to the carriage house in years." Her voice was steady but hollow, the strain evident. "That was a flat-out lie. He and Ike were supposed to meet there a few hours before Ike stood me up."

"There could be an innocent reason."

But Susanna's voice was flat and serious, and Tess knew they shared the same fear. "What if Richard Montague was the last person to see Ike alive? Wouldn't he want to tell the police, especially now, given the circumstances?''

"Maybe Ike never showed up."

Tess swallowed, her throat dry and tight. "Maybe he did."

Susanna swore under her breath.

"They meet, they argue over Lauren and Joanna—"

"And Ike ends up buried in the cellar."

Tess looked over at her friend. "Am I getting ahead of the facts?"

"Way ahead." Her green eyes leveled on Tess. "But who cares? You're not a cop. Go sit on the Beacon police, Tess. Make them talk to this Montague character. Look, another month or two of Ike Grantham and I might have been driven to dump him in a dirt cellar myself, but—" She inhaled. "Damn it, you don't get to murder people."

And there it was, Tess thought. You don't get to murder people.

She printed out a copy of the pertinent e-mails and charged out, promising Susanna she'd check in later. "Don't tell your grandmother or *anyone* who's ever stepped foot in my father's bar about this development, okay? I could be off track, and it was hard enough explaining falling on top of a skeleton in the first place."

Susanna nodded, but managed a grim smile.

"Davey and the gang would never let you live down accusing someone of murder based on an e-mail."

"God, it is thin, isn't it?"

"Go. Let the police talk to Montague and find out if he has a simple explanation."

"I hope he does. Matter of fact, I'm still hoping it *was* a ghost I saw."

Susanna said nothing, but Tess knew—they both knew.

Ike Grantham was dead.

Andrew found Lauren in her herb garden with her poodles. The little dogs were running through the grass, looking as if they'd collide, but never did. Lauren stood on a narrow gravel path among the herbs—Andrew recognized oregano, several kinds of thyme, sage, all getting going for the season. The seaside mansion and extensive grounds reminded Andrew that Lauren Grantham Montague was a wealthy woman. It was easy to forget, and maybe she wanted it that way. She didn't have drivers or guards at a gate or even full-time household help, but she came from money—and a lot of it.

If she or Ike wanted to disappear, or to make someone else disappear, they could do it.

"Dolly would enjoy the poodles." Lauren spoke without looking at him, her gaze on the dogs. "You should bring her by sometime."

One of the dogs scrambled over Andrew's foot.

He ignored the tight ball of tension in his gut and concentrated on why he was here. But he let her have her moment of pleasantries. Why not? "I'm sure she'd get a kick out of these guys. She's an animal lover."

Lauren turned to him, her eyes red-veined, as if she hadn't slept in days. She smiled without feeling. "Most princesses are."

Her comment irritated him. Her idea of being a princess and Dolly's were so different. Lauren didn't have a clue about how he or his daughter thought. It wasn't because she was rich. That was too simple, too black-and-white. She established her own ideas for who people were and what they believed, why they did what they did, to suit herself. She'd take one fact about them and run with it, creating a whole panorama out of one tidbit. He'd seen her do it even with antiques she brought to Harl. She'd mix fact with fantasy, project herself and her own perceptions and beliefs, and turn a Windsor chair into a grand story.

Bottom line, she tended to jump to conclusions about people.

Andrew suspected she had about him.

"Tess Haviland's skeleton is for real," he said.

She didn't seem surprised at his abrupt comment. "She thinks it's Ike. That's the police's nightmare scenario. They're hoping he turns up."

"What about you?"

She shrugged. "It would be horrible if it was Ike. I'd suffer personally, of course, but so would the project, my husband, you. Richard's Pentagon appointment is already in jeopardy, just at the whiff of something wrong. And you. You're right next door. Can you imagine if it turns out that Ike Grantham was killed in the Thorne carriage house?"

"You sound like a reporter reading the news. He's your brother."

She tossed back her head, annoyed. "I know who he is."

Andrew didn't back off. "You know more than you've admitted."

She kept her head back, her eyes half-closed as she stared at him. "Do I?"

"Lauren, whatever pieces of this mess you have—maybe you've put them together wrong, come up with the wrong answers."

She scooped up one of the dogs and held it, scratching under its chin. "I think I like dogs better than people." She pressed her cheek to the top of the dog's head, her eyes filled with tears. "You don't respect me, Andrew. You never have. You've never appreciated what I do for you—or anyone else for that matter. You're very independent that way, you know."

He didn't respond. A light breeze had stirred, bringing out the smells of grass and soil, flowers. It was a beautiful spot, no old Adirondack chairs, no overgrown lilacs, no Harl.

Lauren set down the dog and walked a few steps onto the path. The herb garden was planted in a classic star pattern, with a gazing globe at the center. "I haven't seen or heard from my brother since last March. He was supposed to meet Tess that afternoon in Boston to discuss a new design for the project's Web page. They often met up here, but not that day."

The dogs had followed her onto the path and were getting into the herbs. Lauren herded them out of the rosemary. "Stay on the paths, kiddos, or I'll put you inside." She squatted and replaced dirt one of them had scratched up. "He was stopping at the carriage house first. He told me at breakfast. We'd argued."

"About the carriage house?"

She shook her head and rose, brushing the dirt off her hands. "No, about his living arrangements."

Andrew knew what she was talking about. A frequent subject of gossip in town, the Grantham living arrangements were one of their more obvious eccentricities. When he was in town, whether for an extended period or a few days, Ike lived in the family mansion with his sister. It apparently was never a problem with her first husband. He and Lauren had traveled frequently themselves, and his family owned a place on Cape Cod. After their divorce, with their daughter away at school, it was just Ike and Lauren again, brother and sister, in the Beacon by the Sea house where they'd grown up, an arrangement that apparently had suited them.

But Andrew guessed all that changed when Lauren decided to remarry. "Richard didn't want Ike staying here?"

"He wanted me to buy out Ike's share, minus all the work I'd had done, the maintenance, the taxes I'd paid. If not for me, the termites or the tax man would have gotten this place. Ike never lifted a finger or contributed a dime. Richard didn't want to be unfair to him, but Ike was furious. You know how he was—is." The correction was halfhearted, and she gave a quick, sad smile, as if she didn't expect Andrew to believe she thought her brother was alive. "Rules and details like mowing the lawn and paying property taxes were for other people, not him. He was above that sort of day-to-day trivia. That's all well and good, I told him—then he should hire someone to handle the tasks that bore him."

"I don't recall you two arguing in the time I've known you."

"We never did, but Richard made me see how my brother was taking advantage of me—and had been for years and years. All our lives, really."

Andrew walked onto an offshoot of the main path, two of the dogs scooting past him. He was suddenly aware of the stillness and beauty around him and expected this would be hard to give up. And Ike would feel entitled to it. That was the way he was.

But Andrew stuck to the main issue—Ike's actions on that day in March. "Why was he headed to the carriage house?"

"Oh, he was being ridiculous. He said he never should have given it to Tess, he should have kept it himself and renovated it as his Beacon-by-the-Sea home. He was trying to pretend nothing I said mattered."

"The carriage house isn't on as grand a scale as this place—"

She waved a hand angrily. "Ike was just blowing smoke. He'd never give up this place without a fight, without making me feel as if I were stabbing him in the back. He'd fight me every inch of the way. I never told Richard, but according to our parents' will—he could win."

"They stipulated you both owned the property or neither did?"

She nodded, almost embarrassed. "Basically. It was a way to manipulate me from the grave. They knew Ike wouldn't live up to his share of the responsibilities, so they made sure I'd have to keep sweeping up after him the way they did. It's not as if I couldn't afford to." She turned and started back down the path toward the lawn, walking slowly, pensive more than outraged. "Richard was having none of it. I didn't want him to know how I rated with my parents.''

"What did you do after you and Ike argued?" Andrew asked.

"I went to the office. Ike got all the prestige there, too, without having to do any of the hard work. He did what he wanted to, what amused him. I was furious with myself for putting up with it. It was as if Richard had taken off the blinders, and I have to say I didn't thank him for it. It's an awful feeling, knowing you've been a doormat for your brother, that your own parents expected that of you.''

Andrew headed on a parallel path back out to the lawn, the poodles there ahead of him, finally collapsing in the shade. "You must have hated him at that moment," he said.

"No, that's just it." She smiled over at him, tears spilling out onto her cheeks now. But her voice was steady, as if she was unaware she was crying. "I loved my brother. I take him as he is, faults and all, the whole package. All I really wanted, I realized, was the same from him. Acceptance of my bad points, appreciation for my good ones.''

"So, you're sitting in your office, fuming, but finally you figure—the hell with it, I need to patch things up with Ike, explain to Richard my brother's a part of the package and move on.'' Andrew glanced over at her. "You don't wait. You head to the carriage house.''

"Yes." Her voice was distant, and he could feel her transporting herself back in time, to that March day. "It was very cold. I remember being impatient for spring. March is my least favorite month, but last year it was just interminable. But I walked over. I wanted the cold air to whip the last of the resentment out of me, I suppose."

"What time?"

"It was before lunch. About eleven, I'd say."

She spoke in a monotone, and she began shivering. Andrew stepped closer to her. "Then what?"

"I didn't see his car. He must have walked. He was always so physical, and he'd have wanted the exercise after our argument. I knew he was there." She crossed her arms on her chest, pressed them against her. "I climbed up the side steps."

She stopped, her face going ashen, the shivering worse. Andrew knew he had to keep her in that moment, talking. "Did you go inside?"

"Not then."

"You saw something," he said.

Her eyes met his. He could see her swallow. "I saw you."

"You're sure?"

"You were going through the lilacs. You had on that old denim jacket of yours. I called you, and you didn't answer."

"Did you see me, Lauren, or did you see my jacket?"

"I saw *you*."

He didn't argue, still wanted her in that moment. "What did you do after you didn't get an answer?"

"I went inside."

"Into the carriage house," he prodded.

She nodded, her eyes dry now, dull. "There was water...and an awful smell. Lime. Flesh. At first I thought it was my imagination—"

"You thought it was the ghost at work."

"Yes, the ghost. That's what I thought. But I knew..." She looked at him, focused on him. "I knew better."

"Lauren—"

But she didn't stop, and he saw what was coming, felt it. "I knew you'd killed my brother. Because of Joanna. I didn't blame you. Ike shouldn't have gotten involved."

He didn't react outwardly. Carefully, he took her back to that day last March. "When you were at the carriage house, did you see Ike?"

"No." She shook her head. "Not then. The trapdoor was wet. It—it was unlatched. I latched it again and left. I never went back."

"You went back this Saturday," Andrew said quietly.

"Yes, when Tess finally showed up. I couldn't bring myself to act any sooner. I wish I'd waited until later in the evening, but Richard—" She paused to swallow, her breathing light and rapid, her voice strangely calm. "Richard would have noticed and asked questions. Andrew, I didn't want you to realize what I knew. I just wanted to take care of Ike for you."

Jesus, Andrew thought, but maintained his outward control. "You collected his remains from the carriage house cellar."

"So you didn't have to."

"Where are they now?"

With one hand, she brushed back her straight, shining hair and leveled her eyes at him. They were clear and sad, but also, Andrew decided, a little smug. After all, she'd risked a lot to do him this favor. "I'll show you. We'll need to decide what to do with them."

We. Andrew gritted his teeth. Had someone tried to frame him? Or was connecting him to the jacket just a leap of logic on Lauren's part? She got a glimpse of denim and filled in the blanks.

She started across the lawn and glanced back at him, not breaking her stride. "Ike always wanted to be buried at sea." She smiled almost peacefully. "I think we can arrange that, don't you?"

Andrew decided it was time to go on record. "Lauren, I didn't kill him."

But she ignored him, whistling for the poodles. They roused, stretched and trotted after her with less energy than they'd romped in the herbs.

"Coming?" she asked, the wind picking up, whipping tawny hairs into her mouth.

Andrew nodded. "Sure."

She took him around front to the driveway. Her car was parked in front of his, and he winced as she went to the trunk. "Hell," he breathed, watching her pop it open.

She gasped. *"No!"*

Andrew saw from where he stood. The trunk was empty.

This woman had been carrying her brother's remains in her trunk for the past three days, thinking Andrew had killed him.

She spun around at him. "Is this your idea of a *joke?* He was in a black garbage bag. I put him there myself. I made sure I had all of him. I didn't want to leave behind a finger or something for the police to find. You know, with DNA testing, these days you can't just leave that sort of thing lying around." She was talking rapidly, her composure eroding fast. "My God in heaven. What kind of person would steal a bag of *bones* out of my car?"

What kind of person would have them in there in the first place? Andrew reined in an urge to get in his car and get the hell out of there. "Lauren, we need to call the police."

She frowned at him. "What?"

"I didn't kill Ike. You don't need to protect me."

"But I—I saw you."

"It wasn't me."

She blinked. "What?"

He was losing her. The stress of finding her trunk empty was too much. "Where's your husband?"

"Richard? He's at work."

Andrew didn't think so. Richard Montague was shorter than he was and thicker through the chest, but he could have easily grabbed the denim jacket off its hook on the back porch and thrown it on, just in case someone saw him at the carriage house and Ike's body was discovered sooner rather than later.

Even later—now, over a year later—his simple precaution was paying off.

"Lauren, did you tell Richard you were going to the carriage house to talk to Ike that morning last March?"

She rallied. "Yes, we talked right after I got to the office. Why?"

Because it meant Richard had planned for her to think Andrew had killed her brother, in case she showed up. He'd guessed how she'd react. He was an expert in that sort of thinking. It also meant killing Ike wasn't an accident Richard covered up, but a deliberate act.

"We need to call the police," Andrew said. "And we need to find your husband."

Twenty-Five

—❧❦❧—

Richard needed a murderer.

He parked his car in the carriage house driveway. He had the outlines of a plan—a daring plan, because daring was called for—and he needed to be direct. To hide his car was to invite the wrong sort of question.

He was an innocent man. He needed to act innocent.

He got his Walther .9 mm out of the glove compartment. Lauren hated guns, so he'd never mentioned the one he kept in his desk at his office. It was against company policy, but he'd sneaked it in piece by piece.

He tucked the weapon into his waistband and got Ike's bones out of the trunk. With the bag tightly sealed, no smells could escape, yet he could smell it, anyway, knew it was the memory of over a year ago. He hadn't expected blood. Ike must have caught his head on a loose nail on his way down the carriage house stairs.

But there was the smell of the lime, too, it and the dirt cellar floor, Ike's body, all wet and slick from being hosed down. He'd had to speed decomposition, move things along before warm weather set in.

He'd burned Ike's expensive clothes and tossed the ashes into the sea. Much easier than getting rid of a body. He'd cleaned up inside as best he could.

He hadn't worried that much about someone discovering Ike's remains in the cellar. He'd taken precautions. But he hadn't counted on Lauren stealing them. He thought he could weather having a brother-in-law turn up dead, but having his wife involved was something else altogether. That smug bastard Jeremy Carver would never stand for that sort of scandal.

No, he couldn't just dump Ike's remains at sea. He needed to produce a murderer. An ending to this sordid affair. The work he did was far too important to risk that he might end up in any way tarnished by Ike Grantham's death.

He ducked through a small gap in the lilac hedge, the trash bag snagging on a branch. The smell came through, musty and earthy. His stomach roiled.

He could hear the little girl—Dolly—singing in her tree house. He moved quietly across the lawn to Harley Beckett's workshop. The door was open, and as he crossed the threshold, he removed the Walther from his waistband and leveled it at Harl, who was already reaching for a baseball bat.

"I wouldn't," Richard said.

"Yeah, you wouldn't—you've got a goddamn gun. What do you need with a baseball bat?"

But Harl's hand was suspended midair, his eyes focused on Richard, his white ponytail hanging over his left shoulder. Richard set the bones on the floor. "With Tess Haviland's report of a skeleton, I've reluctantly come to the conclusion that you had to be involved. You live right here on the other side of the lilac hedge. You're a burnout. There was no love lost between you and my brother-in-law. But before I went to the police with such an explosive accusation, I thought I should check it out myself. Armed, of course."

"Just don't touch the kid. You hear me? Touch her, and I'll haunt you forever. It won't be pretty."

Richard smiled and shook his head. "Such a romantic." He motioned toward the door with his gun. "Shall we? I'm afraid I need you at the carriage house."

"Hide the weapon. I don't want Dolly to see it. I'll cooperate."

"Just move," Richard said, "and pray."

The little girl didn't stop singing as Richard followed Harl back through the lilacs. Beckett seemed to relax once they were onto the carriage house driveway, out of view of the tree house. He glanced back at Richard, his eyes knowing. "No way I'm coming out of this alive?"

"Unfortunately, no," Richard said. "No way. It's not personal. In my work I've learned that sometimes one must make sacrifices for the greater good."

"The greater good here being saving your sorry ass."

"The world needs me."

"Yeah? You know what I say? Screw the world."

Richard smirked. "That's what all the burnouts say. Let's go inside, shall we?"

Harl started up the kitchen steps.

"You're a brave man," Richard said. "There's a role in the world for simple, uneducated, brave men with a clear sense of duty."

"It's called cannon fodder."

"Gallows humor?"

Beckett didn't answer.

Once inside, Richard had him unlatch the trapdoor and lift it. "I know you're going to try something. In fact, I'm counting on it."

But what Beckett did, Richard hadn't counted on. He said, "Fuck you," and dove headfirst through the trapdoor. He might have been diving into the ocean.

Richard fired, striking Harl in the hip as he disappeared through the opening. His second shot hit the wall. He heard Harl land with a sickening thud on the dirt floor below, without a cry of pain, a moan or even so much as a sigh.

Richard stood over the dark opening. Maybe Harl had broken his neck. A headfirst dive was risky and awkward—unexpected. But if he'd gone through the trapdoor feet first, Richard would have had a better chance of hitting a vital organ or shooting him in the head. It didn't matter, provided Richard could credibly claim self-defense.

What a moronic move on Harl's part, Richard thought, frustrated, as he got down on his knees and with his free hand, unlatched the ladder. He had to make sure Harl was dead. The only way his plan would work was if he could claim to have killed Harley Beckett in self-defense.

Though who would believe Beckett's version of events over his own?

The ladder dropped to the floor.

This was very risky. If Harl was alive and functioning, Richard would be exposed on the rickety ladder.

Best to go around to the bulkhead, he decided.

He tucked the Walther into his waistband, observed that he wasn't breathing hard at all and headed for the kitchen door.

A little girl popped through the lilacs. "Have you seen my cat?" she asked.

* * *

Tess pulled up in front of Andrew's house and jumped out of the car. He wasn't at his office. She'd stopped at the Beacon Historic Project offices to check on Lauren Montague, but she wasn't there, either. Tess wanted to talk to both Lauren and Andrew about her visit to the police.

They were looking into Ike Grantham's disappearance. They weren't happy with what they'd found—or, more accurately, *hadn't* found—so far. They thought perhaps she had seen a skeleton on Friday night after all.

"We wish you'd called us then," Paul Alverez had told her.

"I wish I had, too."

She pounded up the front steps, but the door was locked and no one answered the bell. She went around back, calling for Harl and Andrew both.

Harl's workshop door was open. Tess picked up her pace, calling for him as she ran over to the outbuilding at the far end of the yard.

She saw the black trash bag and knew what it was. To be sure, she tucked a finger in where it was torn and peered inside.

Bones.

Ike.

It was after school. Harl would have picked up Dolly by now. Had they gone somewhere together?

"Dolly!"

Tess ran out of the shop, climbed up into the girl's

tree house. There were stuffed animals and her tea set and books, and a plate of chocolate chip cookies.

"*Dolly!*"

She could hear panic edging into her voice, assaulting her system. She half climbed, half jumped out of the tree house. She had to call Andrew, but she'd left her cell phone in the car.

Tippy Tail leaped out of the rhododendrons. Tess was so startled, she thought she'd die on the spot, but she didn't scream.

Someone had put the garbage bag in Harl's shop. Not Harl, she thought.

If Tippy Tail had escaped from the pantry and her kittens, Dolly would be on the case. *Find her,* Tess told herself. *Then call the police.*

Or call the police first?

She was already at Dolly's gap in the lilac hedge. A fat blossom brushed against her face as she started through to her yard.

A black BMW was parked in her driveway. A painful jolt of adrenaline shot through her. *Richard.* Tess took a step backward, knowing she had to call the police now, first, but she heard Dolly say, "My name's *Princess* Dolly."

Tess went dead-still.

Oh, God.

Her only advantage was that they hadn't seen her. She had no choice. She had to back out into Andrew's yard, and she had to call him, and she had to call the police. She couldn't take any chances. Not with a six-year-old, she thought. Not with Dolly.

"And I'm *not* going into that dirty old cellar!"

She was there in the lilacs before Tess could move, and the little girl gasped in surprise. "Tess! Tell that man I don't have to do what he says. Have you seen Tippy Tail? And I can't find Harl." She was talking rapidly, ready to cry. "Will you help me find Tippy Tail and Harl?"

Richard Montague came up behind Dolly. "Hello, Miss Haviland."

Tess grabbed the little girl, pulled her through the lilacs and shoved her toward the house. "Run, Dolly! Run! Go get your dad. Hurry!"

"But what are you—"

"Go! It's an emergency. Get your dad. Call 911. Tell them Richard Montague's a—a—"

Dolly's eyes widened in terror. "Is he a bank robber?"

"Yes!" Tess hung on to every shred of control, refused to look back through the lilacs, although she knew what was happening. Dolly was moving toward the house. "Show me how fast you can run!"

Dolly started screaming and running.

"Oh, for God's sake." Richard Montague leveled a very black gun at Tess through the gap in the lilacs. "Obviously you're in this with Harl."

Tess feigned complete surprise, as if Montague

couldn't have heard her instructions to Dolly. "Look, I don't know what you're talking about. Is Harl with you? I can't believe he left Dolly alone."

"Come through the lilacs, Miss Haviland."

She really had no choice. While she had her doubts whether he'd shoot her—how would he explain it?—he just might. "Fine," she said, impatient, ignoring the twist of fear in her stomach, "let's get this straightened out. I don't like people pointing guns at me."

When she landed on the carriage house side of the lilacs, Richard Montague stepped back. He looked ragged, gray-faced. And calm, she thought. Arrogant. "I don't usually underestimate people," he said, "but I'm afraid I underestimated Harley Beckett."

"Harl? Come on. He works on furniture and takes care of a six-year-old."

"And you," Montague added, as if she hadn't spoken.

"Me? Not to worry. People underestimate me all the time. It comes with the turf. When you're a graphic designer, the artists all think you're not a real artist and thus not one of them, and the non-artists all think you're a real artist and thus not one of *them*." She sighed, her instincts operating almost without her consent. "Please put the gun away. I'm not in cahoots with Harley Beckett."

"He's manipulated everyone, my wife included.

He killed Ike. I found his remains in the trunk of Lauren's car. I brought them here—I was furious, I admit. I wasn't thinking.''

Tess doubted Richard Montague ever stopped thinking. "You confronted him?"

He nodded. "I should have called the police."

"But you didn't. What did Harl do?"

"He told me he wanted to confess. We walked over here together, but that was another manipulation. He jumped me, and my gun went off—"

"My God." Tess could feel herself go pale, her breathing get shallow. Her throat and chest felt tight. "Were either of you hurt?"

"I wasn't."

"Dr. Montague—"

"You've done well, Tess, but now—" He shrugged, resigned. He motioned at her with his gun. "Let's go inside, shall we?"

Richard didn't love her. He'd never loved her. He loved the *idea* of her. Her money. Her family name. Her house on the ocean. Ike had seen through him from the beginning.

She should have known. He saw through everybody.

Lauren ducked under a low-hanging branch and sank onto her favorite teak bench under a canopy of climbing roses. They wouldn't bloom until mid-

June. She wondered if she'd be around when they did.

What did the police do to a woman who'd tried to cover up the murder of her brother, even if she was protecting the wrong man?

Would she be arrested, tried, found guilty of something and thrown into prison?

If she'd testified against Andrew, he could have been convicted, like Jedidiah Thorne, of a murder he did not commit.

But, of course, Andrew would never lose control. She should have known.

Two poodles climbed onto her lap, the third snuggled next to her. She sank her head back and closed her eyes, smelling the roses that weren't there as she waited for the police to come for her.

The police were on the way.

Andrew gripped the wheel of his truck and drove along the ocean road. The tide was up, the wind brisk. He had his windows rolled down and was breathing in the ocean smells, letting them calm him. He would get home. He would find Harl and Dolly.

Harl wasn't answering his phone, but he did that on a regular basis.

But not today. He'd answer today. He had to.

Andrew hit redial on his cell phone one more time. A little farther and he'd be there.

Dolly.

He jumped on the brakes and was out of his truck before the picture fully registered in his brain. His daughter. She was running down the side of the road, red-faced, her sturdy little legs eating up pavement.

He scooped her into his arms. She was sweating, unable to talk or cry.

"I've got you, baby, I've got you."

"The bank robber," she choked out. "The bank robber."

"I know, I know."

She gulped. "Tess."

He wanted to tell her it would be okay, but he didn't know it would be. He carried her to his truck, kept her on his lap as he climbed behind the wheel and pulled the door shut.

"Are they at the carriage house?" he asked softly, trying to sound calm, in control, to hide his own terror.

She nodded, holding on to him tight.

Then his house was safe.

He dialed the police and told them Richard Montague might have hostages at the carriage house.

His truck moved forward, down the road. Dolly's sweat soaked into her shirt. And his own.

She began to cry openly. "Daddy, Daddy, Tippy Tail's *gone*."

"She'll come back, Dolly. She won't leave her babies."

And his heart wrenched, Joanna's voice playing back to him. *"I'll be back, Dolly. I would never leave my baby."*

Ah, Joanna, he thought. You died too young, and I'll be forever sorry for that.

But every fiber of his being, right now, with his daughter in his arms, was with Tess. He couldn't lose her.

He pulled to a stop in front of his house.

Harl staggered in front of the truck. A baseball bat dangled from one hand. He was ashen-faced, his entire front covered in dirt, his face smeared with it.

And blood. It was on his hands and arms, and Andrew saw the dark, wet spots on his jeans and black POW-MIA shirt.

As Andrew opened the truck's door, Harl grabbed Dolly. "Go," he told Andrew. "I just crawled out of the carriage house bulkhead. Montague's there. Go before the son of a bitch—" But Dolly was staring at him, wide-eyed, and his voice softened instinctively. "I've got you, sweetie." His eyes, pain-wracked but totally focused, leveled on Andrew. "Don't wait. Go."

Andrew took the baseball bat and went.

"I think that cat wants to move her kittens back here." Tess spoke matter-of-factly, ignoring the panic that was trying to work its way through her, ignoring the gun. Richard had told her it was a

Walther .9 mm. She'd told him she didn't know guns. "Did you shove Harl through the trapdoor the way you did Ike?"

Richard had quit his it-was-Harl act. He was thinking—plotting his strategy, she knew—before he killed her rather than after. He had the trapdoor open already.

"Don't you think you should make sure Harl's dead first?"

She thought that would buy her some time. If he wasn't dead—and she prayed constantly he wasn't—he might have a chance to do something to help their critical situation. And if he was dead, she knew he wouldn't want Richard Montague to get away with another murder.

If he did, they could haunt the damn carriage house together. Her, Harl and Jedidiah.

Don't get giddy. Stay focused!

"Tess! Montague!" Andrew was yelling from the driveway in that hell-to-pay voice. "The police are on their way. For God's sake, Montague, cut your losses. Harl's alive."

In that split second between thinking he had the upper hand and realizing he didn't, Richard Montague gave Tess the opening she'd been waiting for. It was a gesture, a momentary loss of concentration, but she saw it, knew it.

And she gave him a slicing, unequivocal kick to

the testicles, just the way Davey Ahearn had taught her.

Montague dropped the Walther down the trapdoor and sank forward in agony, and Tess followed with another kick, throwing him off balance. He stumbled, falling into the dark opening, grabbing the ladder with one hand as he cursed and spat.

She stomped on his hand.

In a fight, her godfather had always told her, you don't show mercy. But you fight to get away, period.

Montague let go, but before he could regain his balance, Tess slammed the trapdoor shut, latched it and ran out through the kitchen.

The police were massing in her driveway, lights and sirens off.

But she landed in Andrew's arms.

"Perfect timing," she said, her voice catching.

He managed a ragged smile. "Always."

Twenty-Six

It was chowder night at Jim's Place.

Davey Ahearn was on his stool at the end of the bar, and the Red Sox were playing an away game with an expansion team he didn't consider worthy of the big leagues. Tess didn't even know who it was. She was concentrating on her chowder and her argument with her father.

"The carriage house is on the state historic register," she said. "I can't do a deck with a giant hot tub. Besides, that's tacky."

"Almost getting yourself killed—that's tacky."

It had been a month. Four weeks of no skeletons, beautiful spring weather, and time with Andrew and Dolly. First, they'd made sure the six-year old was okay. Rita Perez was a huge help, and Tess could see Harl was falling in love with the ex-nun. She'd done her part, too, because she'd once been a trau-

matized six-year-old girl and could talk to Dolly in
a way the little girl understood.

But Dolly was resilient and creative, and a step
in her healing, Tess thought, was moving from the
world of royalty to oceanography. She was loading
up on stuffed penguins, whales, dolphins and sea
otters. But cats were still her favorite, and she'd
even managed to talk her father and Harl into keeping one of the kittens, the gray one, Cement Mixer.
Tippy Tail had settled in and no longer ran off for
long stretches.

Tess had settled in, too, if not in Andrew's house
at least in his life, and that both scared and excited
her. It meant walks on the beach with him, wine on
the back porch, fixing dinner together, working in
the yard together, coming up with ideas for the carriage house together. And dates. Once Dolly was in
good shape, Tess had pointed out that uncovering a
murder and stopping a murderer didn't count as a
date.

She'd spend nights in the guest room or at her
apartment, never at the carriage house, never in Andrew's room, not until one night when Dolly was
off with Rita Perez, Harl and the rest of the Thorne
family in Gloucester, celebrating his release from
the hospital.

Tess remembered every slow, delicious move Andrew made that night in his bed as they made love,
the feel of his rangy, muscular body, the heat of his

kisses, the look of his eyes in the dark of his bedroom. She remembered quaking with him, losing herself with him.

But thinking of such things in her father's bar could only lead to trouble. "If not for Davey, you know," she said, "I might have ended up dumped through that trapdoor myself."

Her father shook his head. "Damn, I never thought I'd hear my daughter tell me she was alive today because Davey Ahearn taught her how to kick a man in the balls when she was twelve years old."

"Best time to learn," Davey said.

Jim Haviland took her empty bowl and refilled it, not waiting to be asked. He'd also made chocolate cream pie, her favorite, because he knew she'd be here tonight. Tess understood. It was his way of telling himself she'd come through this mess intact. She was alive. Richard Montague was awaiting trial, and Lauren, both shattered and relieved by the truth of what happened to her brother, had her lawyers working out a plea bargain for her role in covering up Ike's murder.

A slim, yellowed volume had turned up in Tess's mail at work. Adelaide Morse's diary. There was no note, but Tess knew it must have come from Lauren. She'd read it in one sitting. Jedidiah Thorne was innocent. He didn't kill Benjamin Morse, yet he'd refused to mount a defense at his trial—because the evidence against him was too overwhelming and he couldn't win without a confession from Adelaide? Or because of that peculiar sense of Thorne honor Tess had come to know so well? She'd given the diary to Andrew. He could correct the public, historic record. Or not.

"I don't know how you can draw up plans for that damn place," her father said. "I'd tear it down."

"I can't. It's on the historic register."

Davey grunted. "One match. That's all it'd take."

"Look, I don't expect you two to understand, and I'm not sure I do myself, but something happened…" Tess sighed, scooping up more chowder. It was thick and creamy, a pat of butter melting into the clams and potatoes. "About a week after the police took Montague away, I'd been to see Harl in the hospital. He was trying to break out, but Rita Perez, Dolly's teacher, was there. Anyway, I stopped back at the carriage house."

"By yourself?" her father asked.

She nodded. "The bad guy was in jail."

"Up to me, you'd never go out alone again," he grumbled. "So, what happened?"

"I was standing in the big room, picturing Ike falling to his death, Richard Montague shooting Harl as he dived through the trapdoor, me fighting him off. I could see Dolly running through her yard, screaming in total panic. I could feel my chest squeezing, a panic attack coming on."

"I don't believe in panic attacks," Davey said. "I think that's a bunch of pop-psych bullshit."

Tess cast him a silencing look.

"Go on," her father said.

"Then—I know this is going to sound weird—but it's what happened. I felt this warmth surround me, this incredible sense of peace, and I knew it was Jedidiah and Ike...and Mom," she said. "They were there, all of them. And I knew it would be all right."

For two seconds, Davey and her father were silent, and she thought for once in her life, they might actually understand her creative imagination.

Then Davey snorted. "Hell, I wish I had me some ghosts today to tell me it was all right, I could open the trap on that sewer line and all those weeping-willow roots would just melt away. Uh-uh. Broke my goddamn plumber snake on them."

"I was going to get rid of my trapdoor," Tess said, "but I don't think so. I think I'll keep it around for you, Davey. You bug me, and I'll give you a good kick to the testicles—"

"Balls," he said. "Testicles sounds too medicinal."

"I'm not even going there."

"Chowder night, the Red Sox and a discussion of ghosts and men's privates." Andrew slid onto the stool next to her and grinned. "My kind of place."

Tess felt a surge of warmth and glanced over at

Davey, wondering if he'd noticed. But she didn't care. She smiled at Andrew. "How long have you been here?"

"An hour."

"An *hour?*" She glared at her father. "You knew? Is this some male thing, you not telling me he was here? Because it has to stop."

He shrugged. "You've got eyes. You can see who's here as well as I can."

"I was preoccupied."

"With fantasizing about turning a haunted carriage house into a graphic design studio," Davey said. "Geez, Thorne, I'm glad you came forward before my eyes glazed over in boredom. You're the architect. You like this stuff."

Tess kept her focus on Andrew. "Susanna's helping me with a five-year business plan. It's torture for me, but she's having a ball."

"Do you think you can skip chocolate cream pie?" he asked, his voice low, deep, sexy.

"Well, it better be for a good reason—"

"Jesus Christ," Davey said. "You want me to paint you a picture?"

She almost choked.

Her father was grinning. He produced a small stuffed animal from somewhere behind the bar and tossed it to Andrew. "Give that to Dolly. Tell her it's a blue penguin. I picked it up at the aquarium the other day."

Tess was shocked. "Since when are you sneaking off to the New England Aquarium?"

"Since I've had a membership for about a million years. You don't know everything about me, you know." He turned back to Andrew. "The blue penguins are those little guys."

"Thanks. She'll love it." He caught Tess by the arm, sending jolts of sexual energy right through her. "Now, do I have to start a brawl, or are you coming?"

They made it to her apartment, but not as far as her bedroom. She said something about having a drink, and next thing, they'd fallen on her couch, toppling stacks of folded laundry as they tore off the clothes they were wearing.

She felt warm and fit in his arms, her skin smooth and so damn tempting. Andrew knew he'd never get enough of her. Never. With mouth, tongue and teeth, he blazed a trail down her throat and stomach, lower and deeper, wanting to love every part of her, feel her shuddering with pleasure and heat.

But she had ideas of her own, as she always did. Her mouth, tongue and teeth did their own erotic torture, until restraint became impossible.

When they came together, the ferocity of his need was overwhelming. He forced himself to hold back, but she pulled him in deeper, harder, matching his rhythm. Their bodies, minds and souls seemed to melt together, separate, melt again. The release came suddenly, in a blinding, nonstop rush.

Stillness settled in slowly, tentatively. He eased between her and the back of the couch, and she slid in close to him and laid her palm on his chest. "I can feel your heartbeat." She spoke softly, as if she didn't want all of Boston to hear her. "I think it was Jedidiah who put the idea of giving me the carriage house in Ike's head, don't you? A proper ghost would know we belonged together."

"We do, do we?"

"Yes. Absolutely. You, me and Dolly. And Harl. I'm talking to him about moving his shop to the carriage house. He'd have more space. It'd be better for both of us, I think." She sighed, contented. "This will be so much fun."

Andrew smiled at her. She was a strong woman, and she never stopped. That mind was always going. "Work and living arrangements can be worked out. Let's go back to you and me belonging together."

"We do, you know. I think I've known it, on some basic instinctive level, for the past year, and that's why I was reluctant to take possession of the carriage house. I knew I'd have to go through the fires of hell before I could have a man like you. And I did. We did." She smoothed her palms over his shoulders, her eyes fixed on his. "I love you very much, if that's what you're asking."

"I wasn't asking—I was trying to tell you the

same thing." He kissed her softly. "I love you. I want to be a part of your life forever, wherever it takes you."

His cell phone rang, which meant it was Dolly. He rummaged on the floor for it. "Yeah, honey, what's up?"

"Honey?" Harl grunted. "I haven't been called that since I was six months old. Hey, Dolly just threw up. No fever. She's fine. Just wanted you to know."

"Should I come get her?"

"Nah. It was a mechanical thing."

"What did you feed her?"

In the background, he could hear Rita Perez insisting Harl tell him about the sardines. Harl sighed. "She wanted to try sardines. She didn't like them, so she washed them down with some other stuff. Chips and things. You know. Kids."

"I'll be there in the morning. Give her ginger ale. If she gets worse, call me."

Harl swore under his breath. "You'd better get here. She's heaving again. Man. I *told* her the Chinese food would put her over the top."

The line went dead.

Andrew looked at Tess, who was grinning. It was good to see. All the tension of uncovering Ike Grantham's murder had gone out of her. "We have to run up to Gloucester. Harl doesn't do sick kids."

But she was laughing.

He feigned a glower. "And what's so funny?"

"You, me, Dolly and Harl. And Rita Perez. Pop and Davey." She sighed as she rolled off the couch and picked clean clothes out of her scattered laundry. "My life couldn't be better."

He smiled. "Neither could mine."

He crawled into his clothes, and when they walked out into the warm Boston night, he felt it, just the way Tess had described her experience at the carriage house. And he knew.

All his ghosts were at peace.

Harmless prank...or murder?

HELEN R. MYERS

DEAD END

When Brette Barry finds a bloody handprint on a Dead End, she's certain it's a harmless Halloween prank. But when she sends her son over to clean it up, the handprint is gone...and a teenager is missing.

Brette suspects her vindictive neighbors, the Pughs, are involved. The local sheriff is convinced the troubled teen has likely run away again...but he's also suspicious of Sam Knight, Brette's suddenly attentive new neighbor.

Brette can't deny her own doubts about the mysterious man—or her attraction to him. And

> "Ms. Myers gives readers an incredible depth of storytelling."
> —*Romantic Times*

her feelings grow even more conflicted, the truth murkier, when the missing teen reappears, only to confide that they've been searching for the wrong person. *Tracie Pugh* is missing, and the last person to see her alive...was Sam.

New York Times **Bestselling Author**

ELIZABETH LOWELL

GRANITE MAN

Mariah MacKenzie returned to the family ranch to search for a long-lost gold mine in the land of her ancestors. Cash McQueen was a distraction she didn't need, a temptation she didn't want—but the only man tough enough to be her guide on a bold quest for the legendary treasure.

Cash's passion for prospecting didn't run to beautiful women—not after the cruel blow the female species dealt him in the past. Trust wasn't in his vocabulary anymore...until temptation made him want to believe in something more precious than gold....

"I'll buy any book with Elizabeth Lowell's name on it."
—Jayne Ann Krentz

Available February 2001 wherever paperbacks are sold!

Visit us at www.mirabooks.com

MEL810

New York Times Bestselling Author

JAYNE
ANN
KRENTZ

Jamie Garland had fallen in love...with
a lie. Cade Santerre had pretended to
be someone he wasn't. Worse, he'd used
her in his elaborate attempt to catch a
man he believed was a criminal.

Though his suspect had escaped,
Cade was still around, masculine
and overwhelming. He had some
unfinished business and
he needed Jamie's help.
But Jamie had some
unfinished business, as well:
to find out if the man she'd fallen in love
with really existed.

TRUE
COLORS

"Nobody does it better!"
—Romantic Times

Available March 2001 wherever paperbacks are sold!

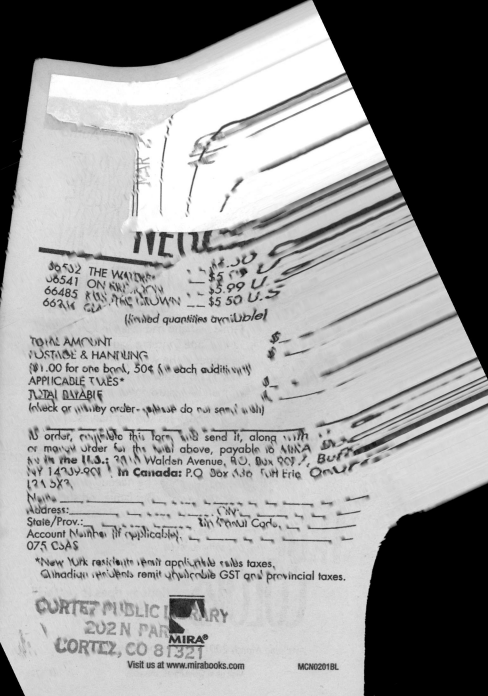

NEW

06502	THE WALDR-	$4.50
06541	ON HIS OWN	$5.99 U.S
66485	KISS THE CROWN	$5.99 U
66216	CLAIM THE CROWN	$5.50 U.S

(limited quantities available)

TOTAL AMOUNT $____
POSTAGE & HANDLING $____
($1.00 for one book, 50¢ for each additional)
APPLICABLE TAXES* $____
TOTAL PAYABLE $____
(check or money order—please do not send cash)

To order, complete this form and send it, along with
a check or money order for the total above, payable to MIRA
Books, to: **In the U.S.:** 3010 Walden Avenue, P.O. Box 9077, Buffalo,
NY 14269-9077; **In Canada:** P.O. Box 636, Fort Erie, Ontario,
L2A 5X3.

Name:_____
Address:_____ City:_____
State/Prov.:_____ Zip/Postal Code:_____
Account Number (if applicable):_____
075 CSAS

*New York residents remit applicable sales taxes.
  Canadian residents remit applicable GST and provincial taxes.

MIRA®

Visit us at www.mirabooks.com   MCN0201BL

CARLA NEGGERS

66582	THE WATERFALL	___ $6.50 U.S.	___ $7.99 CAN.
66541	ON FIRE	___ $5.99 U.S.	___ $6.99 CAN.
66485	KISS THE MOON	___ $5.99 U.S.	___ $6.99 CAN.
66266	CLAIM THE CROWN	___ $5.50 U.S.	___ $6.50 CAN.

(limited quantities available)

TOTAL AMOUNT	$_____
POSTAGE & HANDLING	$_____
($1.00 for one book; 50¢ for each additional)	
APPLICABLE TAXES*	$_____
<u>TOTAL PAYABLE</u>	$_____

(check or money order—please do not send cash)

To order, complete this form and send it, along with a check or money order for the total above, payable to MIRA Books®, to: **In the U.S.:** 3010 Walden Avenue, P.O. Box 9077, Buffalo, NY 14269-9077; **In Canada:** P.O. Box 636, Fort Erie, Ontario, L2A 5X3.

Name:_____

Address:_____ City:_____

State/Prov.:_____ Zip/Postal Code:_____

Account Number (if applicable):_____
075 CSAS

*New York residents remit applicable sales taxes.
Canadian residents remit applicable GST and provincial taxes.

MIRA®

Visit us at www.mirabooks.com

MCN0201BL

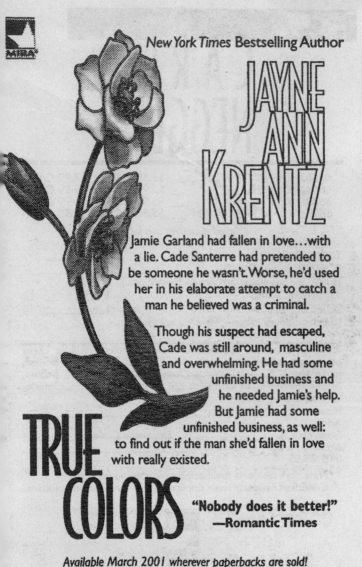

Contents

PART IV:

AMENDMENTS SINCE THE BILL OF RIGHTS

PART V:

THE CONSTITUTION
OF THE UNITED STATES

PART VI:

KNOW YOUR Q'S AND A'S

PART I:

Introduction to the Constitution

What Is Constitutional Government?

People in our country say we live in a democracy (a country where the people govern themselves) or that we live in a republic (a country where people elect officials to govern for them). Both these statements are true. We live in a democratic republic. The type of democracy we have is called *indirect democracy*; that is, we as citizens do not handle the affairs of government ourselves, as is done in a *direct democracy*, but we elect representatives (persons who speak and act for others) to make our wishes known in government.

Our government in Washington, D. C., has a number of different names. It is called the United States government, the central government, the national government, or the federal government. Frequently students are confused by the use of so many different names for the same government.

Our national government (the United States government) is a federal government. The states of the United States make up a federation (a tightly joined group of states giving certain powers, duties, and responsibilities that can best be carried out in the interest of all the states to a central government). So our United States government is also our central government.

Now, we need to know how our federal government gets the power it has and how it is set up to operate effectively and honestly in the interests of the people of the United States.

This information is found in the United States Constitution. Our Constitution is a contract (a written agreement) between the federal government and the people of the states.

Abraham Lincoln in his Gettysburg Address said that ours is a "government of the people, by the people, for the people." More strictly speaking, ours is a government by the *consent* of the people—a government agreed to by the people through a written contract called a constitution.

A document (official paper) of this kind is only as good as the people make it. It must be enforced (carried out) or it becomes meaningless. Some ways that we, as citizens, can make our Constitution effective are: by being well informed as to what our government is doing; by taking an interest in and voting in all elections; by writing letters expressing our opinions to our elected officials; by lobbies (pressure groups in Washington, which try to get laws passed in their interests or keep laws that are against their interests from being passed); by taking court action, in what is called a test case, against any law that we feel is not constitutional; and by petitions (written statements supported by signatures of citizens that are either for or against some action taken or about to be taken by our elected officials).

Seeing that our government operates in the best interests of all the people of the United States is the responsibility of all citizens. We must accept this responsibility to remain a free people and to enjoy the type of government our Constitution enables us to have.

Obviously, even in a democratic republic, everyone cannot be satisfied all the time. Our government is based upon the idea that it should be able to do the most good for the most people most of the time—not that it can always please everybody. Common sense tells us this would be an impossible task.

Our elected officials win their posts by receiving a

majority (more than half) of the votes cast in an election. After every election, there remains a minority (less than half) of the voters whose candidate (person running for office) did not win. Unless a candidate is elected by a unanimous (all for one) vote, there must always be a minority of voters who are not satisfied with the results of the election.

This does not mean that the minority does not have a voice in government. Even though it did not vote for him, the newly elected official is the minority's representative in government, the same as he is the representative of the majority who did vote for him.

A person whose candidate loses must wait until the next election before he may have another chance to try to elect a candidate of his choice to office. In the meantime, it is his duty as a good citizen to accept the wishes of the majority of the voters and cooperate with them. Being a good loser is as important to our democratic republic as being well informed and interested in all activities of our government.

Historical Background of the Constitution

The first plan of national government the United States had was not the Constitution but a plan called the Articles of Confederation and Perpetual Union. The name was soon shortened to the Articles of Confederation by most people. The Confederation (a loosely joined group of states that gives only limited powers to a central government, with each state keeping the most important powers for itself) turned out to be the wrong type of government for the thirteen states that then made up the United States of America. It did not work very well and lasted only a short time. The Articles of Confederation was drawn up in 1777, and the last state did not ratify (agree to) it until 1781. It went out of existence in 1789, when the Constitution was adopted (accepted).

Until the Declaration of Independence was signed in 1776, the states had been under the rule of England, and at the time were fighting the Revolutionary War to remain free. The reason they first chose a confederation was that they were afraid that if the central government was given too much power, they would be trading their newly found freedom for another kind of tyranny (unreasonably harsh rule) of their own making. When the Constitution was adopted, these fears were seen to have been unnecessary, but after their experience with English rule, the states could not be blamed for having had them.

This plan of government called for no central power except an assembly (a gathering of persons). There was no executive (person who sees that the laws are carried out), and there was no judiciary (system of courts).

The assembly was called Congress but had none of the legislative (lawmaking) powers our Congress (national legislature) has today. Congress could not tax (raise money to support the government); it could only ask the states for money. It could not raise an army; it could only ask the states for troops to defend the country. In fact, the members of Congress could not be made to attend meetings, and often so few came that a quorum (number of members that must be present to do business) could not be had. When a quorum could be had, each state had only one vote, regardless of its size, and these votes were meaningless because Congress could not make either the states or individuals obey its commands. It was powerless.

The states were slow to send troops for George Washington's Continental (national) Army; they felt they needed them at home for their own protection. They were even slower to send money to support the government and the army.

After the Revolutionary War, things went from bad to worse. The states began printing paper money that was not backed by gold or silver, and paper money soon became worthless. The states set up tariffs (taxes) on goods crossing their borders, and trade slowed down. Some states even signed treaties with foreign governments.

Thinking men all over the United States began to feel that something had to be done.

In 1787 a convention (meeting) was called in Philadelphia to revise (change and improve) the Articles of Confederation. Delegates (representatives) came from all the states except Rhode Island.

Instead of changing the Articles of Confederation, the delegates, under the leadership of such great Americans as James Madison, Gouverneur Morris, Benjamin Franklin, Alexander Hamilton, and George Washington, decided on a bold new plan—one that no other country had ever tried—to write a constitution setting up a federal government for the states.

This federal government would have three branches: a legislative branch responsible for making the laws; an executive branch responsible for seeing that the laws are carried out; and a judicial branch responsible for explaining the laws and providing just courts of law.

It would also be a government of "checks and balances": each branch is given powers to check (limit) the action of the other two, so that no one branch may become more powerful than the others and attempt to take over the government. This balances (divides evenly), or very nearly balances, the powers of the three branches.

The writing of the Constitution was difficult. There were many opposing ideas as to what should be done. These ideas were settled by compromise (an agreement reached by each opposing side giving in on some points).

The three main issues that had to be compromised were:

1. *The Great Compromise.* The large states wanted representation in Congress to be according to each state's population (the number of people in a given place), while the small states wanted equal representation for each state. This was settled by giving Congress

two houses. The House of Representatives has representation by population, and the Senate has equal representation.

2. *The Commercial Compromise.* To please both the agricultural (farming) southern states, and the industrial (manufacturing and trading) northern states, Congress was given the power to regulate commerce (control trade) with foreign countries and among the states, but Congress could not make laws against bringing slaves into the country before 1808; it could not tax exports (goods being shipped out of a country); and to ratify a treaty (agreement between nations) with a foreign country, a two-thirds vote of the Senate would be needed.

3. *The Three-Fifths Compromise.* The South wanted slaves to count as population toward representation in the House of Representatives. The North did not. This was settled by allowing each slave to count as three fifths of a person. In other words, only three fifths of a state's slaves could be counted as population for the purpose of representation.

Another problem that had to be solved was how to set up a strong federal government and at the same time let the states keep important powers. This was done by dividing the powers of government. Certain powers were to be powers held by Congress only (exclusive federal powers). Some were to be powers held by both state and federal governments (concurrent powers), and other powers were forbidden to either government (denied powers). Any power not mentioned by the Constitution as falling into one of these three groups would be considered powers of the states and of the people.

The writers of the Constitution intended to submit it to the people of the states, rather than to the states' legislatures, to be ratified. In 1787 means of transportation and communication were slow, so as it turned out, constitutional conventions were set up in the states and the people sent delegates to these conventions.

Before the Constitution could become law, it had to be ratified by three fourths (nine out of thirteen) of the states. When it was offered to the people for this purpose, two opposing sides began to form. One group called themselves the Federalists (persons in favor of strong central government), and the other, the Anti-Federalists (persons in favor of keeping strong state government).

As is the American way, each group argued against the ideas of the other and tried to persuade the people to its way of thinking by making speeches and writing in the newspapers. The best known of these writings and perhaps the most important are *The Federalist Papers* by Alexander Hamilton, James Madison, and John Jay, written in favor of the Constitution, and *Lee's Letters from the Federal Farmer to the Republican* by Richard Henry Lee, written against ratifying the Constitution.

These two opposing groups later became the foundation blocks for our first political parties (groups that attempt to control government by winning elections and holding offices).

By July 2, 1788, ten states had ratified the Constitution and it was adopted. It did not go into effect, however, until March 4, 1789, and it was not until 1790 that all the thirteen states had accepted it as the supreme (highest) law of the United States.

CHECK YOURSELF
See if you can fill in the blanks.
Look back for any answer you do not know.

We live in a _____ _____. We as citizens do not handle the affairs of government ourselves, so we live under a system called _____ democracy.

Some other names for the United States government are the _____ _____, the _____ _____, and the _____ _____.

Our Constitution is a _____ between the federal government and the _____ of the states. In other words, we give our _____ to be governed.

To keep our Constitution from becoming meaningless, it is the responsibility of every _____ to see that it is _____.

If after an election, a person finds himself a member of the minority of voters, it is his duty to _____ with the majority of voters, so that our government may continue to run smoothly.

Our first plan of national government was the _____ of _____. It called for a Congress but did not call for an _____ or a _____. Congress had no real power and could only ask the _____ to support the national government. The plan did not work very well, and lasted from _____ until _____.

In 1787 a convention met in _____ to _____ the Articles of Confederation, but instead of changing the Articles of Confederation, the delegates wrote a _____ setting up a _____ government. This was a bold new plan and the only one of its kind in the world.

The _____ _____, the _____ _____, and the _____ _____ were three of the many compromises that were made in the writing of this plan. The powers of government were _____ between the states and the _____ _____.

Constitutional conventions were set up in the _____, and delegates representing the _____ were sent to them. The _____ had to be _____ by _____ _____ of the states before it could become the _____ law of the United States.

A group in favor of ratification was called the _____, and a group against ratification was called the _____. The _____ was adopted in _____ and went into effect in _____.

WORDS YOU NEED TO KNOW

1. **democracy** (a country where the people govern themselves)

2. republic (a country where the people elect officials to govern for them)
3. representative (a person who speaks and acts for others)
4. federation (a tightly joined group of states giving certain powers, duties, and responsibilities that can be best carried out in the interest of all the states to a central government)
5. confederation (a loosely joined group of states that gives only limited powers to a central government, with each state keeping the most important powers for itself)
6. constitution (a contract; a written agreement)
7. supreme (highest)
8. United States Constitution (the supreme law of the United States)
9. lobby (a special interest group, such as doctors, labor unions, businessmen, farmers, or teachers, which tries to get laws passed in its interests or keep laws that are against its interests from being passed)
10. petition (written statement supported by the signatures of citizens that are either for or against some action taken or about to be taken by our elected officials)
11. minority (less than half)
12. majority (more than half)
13. unanimous (all; 100 percent)
14. candidate (person seeking election to office)
15. Articles of Confederation (the first plan of national government in the United States)
16. ratify (agree to; adopt; accept)
17. tyranny (unreasonably harsh rule)
18. assembly (a gathering of persons)
19. legislature (lawmaking body)
20. Congress (our national legislature)
21. executive (person who sees that laws are carried out; an administrator)
22. judiciary (system of courts)
23. taxes (money paid to the government and used for its operation)

24. convention (meeting held for a special reason)
25. revise (change and improve)
26. delegates (representatives)
27. compromise (an agreement reached by each opposing side giving in on some points)
28. population (number of people in a given place)
29. regulate (control)
30. commerce (trade)
31. exports (goods shipped out of a country)
32. treaty (agreement between nations)
33. political party (group that attempts to control government by winning elections and holding offices)

PART **II**:

The Constitution Explained

How the Constitution Is Written

The Constitution was written in its final form by Gouverneur Morris. It is considered one of the most readable and clearly stated documents ever written. A great deal of thought went into the exact wording of the Constitution. It was meant to be easily understood and leave no room for mistaken ideas about what it contained. It is no accident that our Constitution has been amended (added to or changed) only twenty-six times in nearly 200 years and is the oldest living written constitution in the world.

The Constitution contains a "preamble" (an introduction) that states why it was written, a "main body," and twenty-six amendments.

The following simplified text follows the original structure of the Constitution and includes all the information supplied by it, but quite often, by way of explanation, information not found in the Constitution is added.

The Preamble introduces the Constitution by listing six important reasons for writing it:

1. *In order to form a more perfect union*—set up a stronger central government with the states more closely united, so the United States could be one nation, rather than thirteen little countries acting separately as they had under the Articles of Confederation.

2. *To establish justice* (fair treatment)—set up a system of laws and courts that would make all men equal under the law and give all men equal opportunities for fair treatment if accused of a crime.

3. *To insure domestic tranquillity* (peace among the states)—to settle the problems, such as poor trade relations between states, and to prevent open fighting against state governments, as had been the case in Shays's Rebellion against Massachusetts, which was brought about by unfair debt laws.

4. *To provide for the common defense*—to have a strong national army and navy that could defend all the states. If a foreign country attacked any state, it would be defended by a national military force supported by all the states.

5. *To promote the general welfare*—to help provide a higher standard of living for the people of the United States through better government.

6. *To secure the blessings of liberty* (freedom) *for ourselves and our posterity* (future generations of Americans)—to protect the personal rights of all United States citizens for all time.

The main body of the Constitution is divided into seven blocks called articles. Each article is broken down into sections, which list the separate ideas found in that article.

ARTICLE I. THE LEGISLATIVE (lawmaking) BRANCH OF GOVERNMENT
SECTION 1. Congress

All the lawmaking powers of the federal government are given to a body of representatives called the Congress of the United States. Congress has two houses (separate units), the House of Representatives and the Senate.

SECTION 2. The House of Representatives

The members of the House of Representatives serve two-year terms (periods) of office and are elected by those people of the states who are qualified (eligible) voters in the states where they live. Qualified voters in most states must meet these requirements:

1. Be a citizen of the United States.
2. Be a citizen of the state in which they vote (live in the state for a set period of time; from six months to two years, depending on the state).
3. Be eighteen years of age. Originally the states set the age requirement. In most states, twenty-one years of age, but the twenty-sixth amendment sets a uniformly lower age in all states.
4. Be registered (have name put on the official list of qualified voters).

26

Some few states require a literacy (reading and writing) test. Abnormal people, such as idiots and insane persons, persons permanently supported at public expense, and persons guilty of certain crimes are denied the right to vote in nearly all states.

To be a member of the House of Representatives a person must:

1. Be at least twenty-five years of age.
2. Have been a citizen of the United States for at least seven years.
3. Live in the state he is elected to represent. In any state having more than one representative, except New Mexico or North Dakota, he must live in the district (section) of the state he represents.

For the purpose of deciding how many representatives each state may have, a national census (count of the people) is taken every ten years. The first census was taken in 1790 (3,929,214 people) and the last in 1980. Our country now has over 227,000,000 people. The first census did not include Indians, who were not taxed, and counted only three fifths of the slaves as population (as was agreed in the Three-Fifths Compromise). Today everyone is counted.

Originally (when the Constitution was first written) all direct taxes (personal taxes) had to be apportioned (divided) among the states according to each state's population. Since the Civil War there have been no direct taxes other than the income tax and those collected in the District of Columbia. The District of Columbia is governed directly by Congress and is not a state. The income tax is not apportioned according to the states' populations, but this has been provided for by the Sixteenth Amendment to the Constitution.

After the first census there was one representative for every thirty thousand persons in a state, but each state was allowed at least one representative regardless of the size of its population (this protected any state that might have a population of less than thirty thousand persons). Until the time the first census was taken New Hampshire was allowed three representatives, Massachusetts eight, Rhode Island one, Connecticut five, New York six, New Jersey four, Pennsylvania eight, Delaware one, Maryland six, Virginia ten, North Carolina five, South Carolina five, and Georgia three.

In 1929, to keep the House of Representatives from growing too large to work well, Congress passed a law limiting the number of members to 435. When the states of Alaska and Hawaii were admitted to the Union in 1959, a temporary arrangement was made to allow 437 members until the first new Congress met (1963) after the 1960 census was recorded. Congress must meet each year, but Congress is counted as a new Congress each second year because elections are held every two years.

Today we have one representative for about every 521,000 persons.

When a representative from a state dies, resigns (quits), becomes too ill to hold office, or is expelled (removed from office by a two-thirds vote of the other members), the governor of that state must call a special election to fill the vacancy (empty chair) belonging to his state in the House of Representatives.

The House of Representatives chooses its own officers. The Speaker of the House (presiding officer, or chairman, who conducts the meetings), clerk of the House (officer who keeps records of the meetings), parliamentarian (officer who sees that the proper rules of order are followed), chaplain (religious officer), sergeant at arms (officer who may remove unruly persons if authorized by the House to do so), and other less important officers are nominated (named as candidates) by a majority-party caucus (meeting of party leaders to decide candidates). Since the majority party outnumbers the minority party, and every majority-party member is pledged to vote for the candidates his caucus chooses, these candidates are always elected.

The House of Representatives has the sole power (power given to none other) of impeachment (act of accusing a public official of wrongdoing, which may result in his removal from office). A majority vote of the

House of Representatives is necessary to impeach an official.

SECTION 3. The Senate

The Senate of the United States has one hundred members. There are two senators from each state. They serve six-year terms of office, and each senator has one vote.

Since 1913, when the Seventeenth Amendment to the Constitution was ratified, senators have been elected by the people. Before this they were elected by the members of the states' legislatures.

The members of the first Senate were divided as equally as was possible into three groups. The members in the first group were given a two-year term of office, those in the second group a four-year term, and those in the third group a six-year term. After these terms expired (ended), all senators were given a six-year term. This was done so that two thirds of the Senate would always be made up of members with experience in the Senate, and means that every two years, one third of the Senate comes up for election.

The governor of each state was given the power to make temporary appointments (name nonpermanent members) to fill any vacancy in the Senate his state might have, if the state legislature was not in session (meeting). At its next session the state legislature was to elect a new senator. Today (according to the Seventeenth Amendment) the governor of a state may still make temporary appointments to fill vacancies that occur in the Senate from his state, with the state legislature's permission; or he may call a special election to elect a new senator.

To be a senator a person must meet the following qualifications (requirements):

1. Be at least thirty years old.
2. Have been a citizen of the United States for at least nine years.
3. Live in the state he represents.

The Vice-President of the United States is the President of the Senate (presiding officer), but he has no vote except in the case of a tie (equally divided) vote on the floor of the Senate.

All other officers of the Senate, such as president pro tempore (officer who acts as President of the Senate when the Vice-President must be absent, or if the Vice-President becomes President of the United States), chaplain, sergeant at arms, the Senate secretary, and chief clerk are elected by the members of the Senate.

Whereas the House has the sole power of impeachment, the Senate has the sole power of trying impeachment cases. Two thirds of the Senate must be present before the trial may begin, and to convict a public official (declare him guilty of charges made), a two-thirds vote of the senators present is necessary.

If the President of the United States is being tried, the Chief Justice (highest judge of the Supreme Court) presides at the trial. It would be unfair for the Vice-President, who is next in line for the office of President, to preside. President Andrew Johnson was impeached, but was found not guilty (1868). President Richard M. Nixon faced impeachment, but resigned (1974).

The only punishment an impeached official may receive from the Senate is the loss of his office and the loss of the right to ever hold any other office of honor, trust, or profit in the United States government. But if the impeached official has broken any laws, he may be turned over to the regular courts for trial and punishment, the same as any other criminal, once he has been impeached and removed from office.

SECTION 4. Congressional Elections and Meetings

Originally the time, place, and manner of holding elections for senators and representatives were set by the states' legislatures.

Congress kept the right to change, by law, at any time it felt necessary, any rule the states might make in respect to this. Congress has made two changes. In 1842 Congress passed a law stating that representatives be elected from districts within their states, and in 1872, a law that made the Tuesday after the first Monday in November of every even year election day for representatives in every state but Maine. (Since 1957 Maine has also gone to the polls on this day.) One third of the senators is elected on this day as well.

Congress has to meet at least once every year. The first session day is now January 3. The Twentieth Amendment to the Constitution changed it to this date, from the first Monday in December.

SECTION 5. Congressional Rules

Each house of Congress judges the elections, returns, and qualifications of its members. A majority of members makes up a quorum (number of members that must be present to do business). If a quorum is not present in either house, then the members of that house, who are present, may adjourn (stop meeting for a period of time) and force the absent members to attend. Each house may force absent members to attend by using whatever means or penalties (punishments) it has provided to cover this matter.

Each house makes the rules for its proceedings (operations), punishes its members for disorderly behavior, and with a two-thirds vote, may expel (remove) a member. Each house may refuse to let a newly elected member take his seat if a majority of its members decides he cannot qualify for membership.

Each house keeps a journal (record) of what it does from day to day. Each morning Congress is in session, these journals are published in the *Congressional Record*. Any matters that are to be kept secret, such as certain matters concerning our national defense, are left out of the journal. If one fifth of the members present in either house wishes to include in the journal how each member voted in regard to any measure, the vote is recorded in the journal.

While Congress is in session, neither house may adjourn for more than three days without the consent of the other, and both houses must meet at the same place. The Senate and the House of Representatives must work

closely with one another if they are to get anything done.
These two requirements make certain that each house is
always available (close by when needed) to the other.

CHECK YOURSELF
See if you can fill in the blanks.
Look back for any answer you do not know.

The _____ to the Constitution lists these six reasons
for writing it: in order to form a _____ _____
_____; to establish _____; to insure _____
_____; to provide for the _____ _____; to pro-
mote the _____ _____; and to secure the blessings
of _____ for _____ and our _____.

The _____ branch is the lawmaking branch of our
federal government. Our national legislature is called
_____, and it has two _____, the _____ of
_____ and the _____.

A representative must be at least _____ years old,
have been a _____ of the United States for _____
years, and live in the _____ of the _____ he represents. His term of office is _____ years, and the presiding officer of his house is called the _____ of the
_____.

A senator must be at least _____ years old, have
been a _____ for _____ years, and must live in the
_____ he represents. He serves a _____ year term
of office, and his presiding officer, called the _____ of
the Senate, is the _____ of the United States. This presiding officer has no _____ except in the case of a
_____ _____ on the floor. If he is absent, the
_____ _____ _____ acts as chairman in his place.

The number of representatives a state has is determined by its _____. Every state has _____ senators.

The House of Representatives has the sole power of
_____, that is, to bring accusations against a public

official. The Senate has the sole power of _____ these cases. If the President of the United States is on _____, the _____ _____ of the _____ _____ presides. All public officials except congressmen may be _____. Congressmen are _____ by a _____ vote of the members of their own house.

The time, place, and manner in which congressional elections took place were originally left up to the _____ _____. Congress has since set the day for these elections as the _____ following the first _____ in _____ of _____ numbered years.

Congress must meet _____ a year, and the first day of session is _____ _____.

After the election, each house may judge the _____ of its newly elected members and may refuse to seat a member by a _____ vote.

Each house keeps a record of its business in a _____, and each day Congress is in session the information is published in the _____ _____.

Both houses must meet at the same _____ and _____, and neither house may _____ for more than _____ days without the consent of the other.

WORDS YOU NEED TO KNOW

1. Preamble (introduction to the Constitution)
2. union (act of joining together)
3. justice (fair treatment)
4. domestic (pertaining to the home)
5. tranquillity (peace)
6. welfare (well-being; good condition)
7. liberty (freedom)
8. posterity (those who are born after us)
9. term (period of time)
10. register (place name on list of qualified voters)
11. literacy (ability to read and write)
12. congressional district (section of a state that is represented by one member of the House)

13. census (count of the people in any given place—city, county, state, nation, world)
14. direct tax (a personal tax)
15. apportion (divide)
16. resign (quit; give up a job)
17. vacancy (a public office not held by anyone)
18. presiding officer (chairman; person who conducts a meeting)
19. nominate (name as a candidate)
20. caucus (meeting of leaders of a political party held for some special purpose)
21. sole (one; only)
22. impeachment (act of accusing a public official of wrongdoing)
23. impeachment trial (act of deciding innocence or guilt of impeached official)
24. expire (end)
25. appoint (name to take office)
26. temporary (not permanent)
27. session (time spent in meeting)
28. qualification (requirement)
29. originally (at first; in the beginning)
30. quorum (number of members that must be present to carry on business)
31. adjourn (close a meeting until some future date)
32. penalty (punishment)
33. proceedings (manner of performing duties)
34. expel (remove)

IN BRIEF

The two houses of Congress
I. The House of Representatives
    A. Representation by population—435 members
    B. Members serve two-year terms
    C. Chairman is Speaker of the House
    D. Members' salaries
       1. Speaker—$79,125 a year

    2. Other members—$60,662.50 a year
  E. Qualifications for a member
    1. Must be at least twenty-five years old
    2. Must have been a United States citizen for seven years
    3. Must live in state he represents
  F. Members elected by the people in districts of the states they represent

II. The Senate
  A. Equal representation—two members from each state; one hundred in all
  B. Members serve six-year terms
  C. Chairmen are the Vice-President of the United States, who is President of the Senate, and the president pro tempore
  D. Members' salaries—$60,662.50 a year
  E. Qualifications for a member
    1. Must be at least thirty years old
    2. Must have been a United States citizen for nine years
    3. Must live in state he represents
  F. Members elected by people of states they represent

SECTION 6
Congressional Privileges and Restrictions

Senators and representatives receive a compensation (payment) for their services. Their salary is set by law, and they are paid out of the United States Treasury. At the present time congressmen are paid $60,662.50 a year. The Speaker of the House is paid $79,125 a year, the same as the Vice-President of the United States.

In addition to their salaries, congressmen receive free office space, free postage (the frank), free printing for speeches, allowances (set amounts of money for such things as office help, stationery, long-distance telephoning, telegrams, and travel to and from sessions of Congress), pensions (retirement salaries), and income-tax exemptions (certain amount of salaries not taxable). Certain limitations are placed on the amounts allowed in all these cases, and certain conditions must be met in others.

Congressmen have what is known as congressional immunity. A congressman cannot be arrested while attending a session of his house, or while going to or from it, except for treason (making war against the United States, or helping its enemies), felony (a serious crime), or breach of the peace (breaking a law that requires the lawbreaker to appear in court). He cannot be held accountable for any statements he may make against persons in speeches or debates (arguments) in either house. This allows him to speak the truth as he sees it, without fear of having to face a civil suit (court action brought against one person by another) for slander (damaging insults).

No senator or representative may hold any office under the United States government that was created or that had an increase in salary during the time he was in Congress, and no person who holds any other United States government office may be a member of either house of Congress unless he first gives up the other office. This keeps congressmen free from any binding ties with other offices and protects the independence of Congress.

SECTION 7. Passing a Bill

All revenue (tax) bills must originate (begin) in the House of Representatives, but the Senate may amend them. This gives the people a closer check on how they are taxed than they would have if a tax bill could also be introduced in the Senate. Originally the Senate was not elected by the people, but the House of Representatives has always been, and representatives come up for reelection every other year, while senators only come up for reelection after six years.

Any bill, other than a tax bill, may originate in either house.

If a bill is introduced (first brought up) in the House of Representatives and passed by a majority vote, it goes to the Senate, where it must also get a majority vote to be sent to the President of the United States.

The President may sign the bill and make it a law. He may veto (refuse to sign) the bill and return it, with whatever objections to it he may have, to the house where it started. In this case, he would return it to the House of Representatives, where his objections would be read and recorded in the *House Journal*. This time the bill must get a two-thirds vote to be sent to the Senate.

If it gets the needed two-thirds vote in the House of Representatives, it goes, along with the President's objections, to the Senate. If it passes the Senate with a two-thirds vote, it becomes a law without the President's signature. This is called overriding the President's veto. If the bill fails to pass either house with the needed two-thirds vote, it cannot become law. This is called sustaining the President's veto.

This does not mean the idea found in the bill cannot be brought up again. In fact, a similar bill may be introduced in the very next session of Congress.

Any time Congress overrides the President's veto, the names of each member of each house and how he voted —for or against—are recorded in the journal of his house.

If the President neither signs nor vetoes a bill, it becomes a law after ten days—Sundays not counted. If Congress adjourns within that ten days, however, the bill does not become a law. It is automatically vetoed. We call this a pocket veto.

The two houses of Congress have become so large and have so much business that it is impossible for either house to work out the details of all the important bills before it, with all the members acting together. So both houses have a number of committees (groups set up for special purposes), which study bills and recommend (advise) the passage of the ones that they approve.

Every order, resolution (motion), or vote that is required to pass both houses of Congress must be sent to the President of the United States for his approval in the same manner as a bill. If the President does not give his approval, a two-thirds vote of both houses overrides the President's disapproval. This prevents Congress from bypassing the President by calling a bill by some other name.

Some exceptions to this rule are:
1. Adjournment of Congress.
2. Nonlegislative resolutions.
3. Joint (both houses together) resolutions proposing amendments to the Constitution.

CHECK YOURSELF
See if you can fill in the blanks.
Look back for any answer you do not know.

Congressmen are paid for their _____. Members of both houses receive _____ dollars a year in salary. The Speaker of the House is paid _____ dollars a year, the same as the _____ of the United States. In addition to their salaries congressmen receive free _____ _____, free _____, _____ for expenses, and many other benefits.

Except for _____, _____, or _____ of _____, congressmen cannot be arrested when attending or going to or from sessions of Congress. They cannot be sued for anything they say on the floor of either house. These privileges are called _____ _____.

No congressman may hold any office that was _____ or that had an _____ in _____ during the time he was in Congress. No person may be a congressman while holding any other _____ of the _____ _____.

All _____ bills must begin in the House of Representatives. Any other bill may begin in _____ house. If a bill starts in the Senate, it must pass by a _____ vote to go to the House of Representatives, and it must pass the House by a _____ vote to go to the President. The President may _____ the bill and make it a _____, or he may _____ it and return it with his _____ to the house where it began.

To pass a bill over the President's _____, a _____ vote of each house is needed.

If the President neither _____ nor _____ a bill within _____ days, not including Sundays, the bill becomes a _____ without the President's _____. If Congress _____ during this _____ day period, it does not become a _____, and we say the President has used his _____ _____.

Congressional committees _____ bills and _____ the passage of the ones they choose.

Every _____, _____, or vote that must pass _____ houses must be sent to the President. This prevents Congress from bypassing the President by calling a _____ by some other name.

WORDS YOU NEED TO KNOW

1. compensation (payment for goods or services)
2. privilege (special right)
3. restriction (a limitation; control)
4. immunity (protection against)
5. treason (making war against the United States or helping its enemies)
6. felony (a serious crime)
7. debate (argument)
8. civil suit (court case involving a dispute between parties)
9. slander (damaging statements made against a person)
10. revenue (money received from taxation or any other source)
11. bill (a proposed law)
12. originate (begin; start)
13. introduce (bring up; make known)
14. veto (refuse to sign, along with act of returning with objections)
15. objections (reasons for being against)
16. override (pass over)

17. sustain (uphold)
18. pocket veto (President's act of allowing time limit to run out on a bill after Congress has adjourned)
19. committee (group set up for some special purpose)
20. recommend (speak in favor of; advise)

IN BRIEF

How a tax bill becomes a law
1. Usually prepared and introduced by a House committee, but may be introduced by any member
2. Goes to floor of House (may be sent back to committee, for further study and changes, or may not pass)
3. Wins a majority vote in House
4. Goes to Senate (usually sent to a Senate committee to be studied and perhaps amended; if amended, must be returned to House to be passed in new form—in fact, may be sent back and forth until both houses agree on wording of bill; or a compromise may be worked out by a joint committee)
5. Goes to floor of Senate (may be sent back to committee, or may not pass)
6. Wins majority vote in Senate
7. Speaker of House signs
8. President of Senate signs
9. Goes to President (may veto and send back to House with objections—House and Senate may override with two-thirds vote of each house, or may sustain veto; President may neither sign nor veto bill, in which case, becomes law in ten days without his signature; or if Congress adjourns during this time, bill receives pocket veto)
10. President signs
11. Bill becomes law

SECTION 8. Powers of Congress

The "expressed" powers (powers listed in the Constitution) are:

1. Power to lay (raise) and collect taxes (money used to pay expenses of government), duties, imposts (taxes on imports), and excises (taxes on the manufacture, sale, or use of goods within a country) for the purpose of national defense and general welfare of the United States, but all duties, imposts, and excises must be uniform (the same) for all the states.

2. Power to borrow money on the credit of the United States (for example, through the sale of government savings bonds).

3. Power to regulate commerce (control trade), both foreign commerce (trade with another country) and interstate commerce (trade among the states).

4. Power to make naturalization laws (laws that state the requirements a foreigner must meet in order to become a citizen of the United States) and bankruptcy laws (laws that deal with persons or businesses that cannot pay their debts) that are the same for all states.

5. Power to coin metal money or print paper money, to control the value (worth) of both United States money and foreign money to be exchanged for United States money and be spent in this country, and to set up a standard (definite scale) for all weights and measures used in the United States.

6. Power to punish counterfeiters (persons who make imitation money or securities, such as bonds).

7. Power to establish post offices and post roads (federal highways) for the purpose of transporting and delivering mail.

8. Power to encourage progress in science and the arts by passing patent laws (laws that protect the rights of inventors and discoverers) and copy-

right laws (laws that protect the rights of authors, artists, and musicians), so that no one may steal and sell the ideas of anyone who seeks protection for his work under these laws.

9. Power to set up all tribunals (federal courts) inferior (lower in rank) to the Supreme Court, which is set up by the United States Constitution.

10. Power to decide which acts that take place at sea are piracies (thefts) or felonies (serious crimes, such as murder), to make laws to punish these crimes, and crimes against international law (laws that involve most of the countries of the world and that are agreed to by them).

11. Power to declare war, grant letters of marque and reprisal (give civilians licenses to outfit warships at their own expense and fight the enemy; this has not been done since the Civil War) and make rules about captures (men or materials taken from the enemy) on land or sea.

12. Power to raise (sign up men for service) and support (supply) the United States Army, but no appropriation (sum of money set aside for a special purpose) for it can be made except for one two-year period at a time. (It was felt that Congress, by allowing the army money to operate only two years at a time, could keep it from ever becoming so powerful that it might overthrow the government.)

13. Power to set up and supply the United States Navy.

14. Power to make rules for the operation and control of the armed forces, which now includes the United States Air Force, as well as the army and navy. This keeps the military under civilian control.

15. Power to add the states' militias (the National Guard) to the United States military forces, if force is needed to see that a United States law is carried out or to put down insurrection (rebellion) or to defend our country in case of an attack by a foreign country.

16. Power to organize, arm, and make rules for the states' militias; and to have complete control over any militias on active duty with the United States military forces, but each state may appoint the officers and carry on the training of its militia using the discipline (rules and regulations) Congress orders.

17. Power to govern the District of Columbia and the city of Washington (our national capital); and to have full authority (power) over places purchased (bought) from the states for the building of forts, magazines (ammunition storehouses), arsenals (weapons storehouses), dockyards, or any other federal building needed.

The following clause gives Congress its implied powers (powers not listed in the Constitution).

18. Power to make any laws necessary and proper for seeing that the other powers given to Congress, to the United States government, and to any department or officer of the United States government are carried out. This clause is sometimes called the elastic clause because it seems to stretch to fit any situation. But it does not make Congress all-powerful, since the President must see all laws passed by Congress and may veto any he chooses; and since any person in the United States can bring a test case against any law he believes unconstitutional and may take his case as high as the United States Supreme Court.

SECTION 9. Powers Denied Congress

The migration (movement from one place to another) and importation (act of bringing into a country) of slaves could not be prohibited (forbidden) by Congress before 1808, but a tax that did not exceed (not higher than) ten dollars for each slave could be placed on the slave trade.

The privilege of writ of *habeas corpus* (legal paper stating the right of a jailed person to be released if proper charges cannot be brought against him) cannot be suspended (taken away) except during a time of rebellion (war to overthrow the government) or invasion (crossing of our borders by enemy troops), when it might be necessary to suspend it for the protection of the people of the United States. This keeps an arrested person from being thrown in jail and left there without a trial or hearing of any kind.

No bill of attainder (a law that punishes a single individual and denies him the right to a trial) or *ex post facto* law (law making a crime of an act done before the time of making the law) can be passed.

No direct taxes could be collected unless collected in proportion (relation) to the states' population, but the Sixteenth Amendment to the Constitution has changed this by providing for the income tax.

The ports of one state may not be given any advantage in trade over those of any other by regulating commerce in its favor or by making its import taxes less; and goods shipped in the United States by means of water transportation may not be taxed.

No money can be drawn from the United States Treasury without an act of Congress stating how it is to be used. All money collected and spent by the government must be reported in a published account from time to time.

No title of nobility (mark of rank raising a person above other citizens and in some cases above the law) can be given by the United States, and no person holding any public office under the government of the United States may accept any present, emolument (payment), office, or title from any king, prince, or foreign state (nation) without the consent of Congress.

SECTION 10. Powers Denied the States

No state may make a separate treaty, alliance (friendship pact), or confederation; grant letters of marque and reprisal; coin or print money; accept anything but gold and silver money in payment of debts; pass any bill of attainder, *ex post facto* law, or law that might damage the obligation (legal or moral duty involved) of contracts; or grant any title of nobility.

Without the consent of Congress, no state may tax imports or exports except to the extent necessary for the carrying out of its inspection laws, and any money collected beyond the amount for this purpose must be turned over to the national treasury. Congress keeps the right to change or control any of these laws.

Without the consent of Congress, no state may collect any duty on the tonnage (load limit) of ships, keep troops or warships in time of peace, make any compact (agreement) with another state or any foreign country, or fight a war unless it is actually invaded or in such imminent (immediate) danger that delay would be too costly.

CHECK YOURSELF
See if you can fill in the blanks.
Look back for any answer you do not know.

Some of the powers of Congress are: to collect _____; borrow _____ on the _____ of the United States; regulate _____ (both _____ and _____); make _____ laws allowing foreigners to become citizens; coin _____ and decide its _____ and the _____ of foreign _____; fix the _____ of weights and _____; punish _____; set up _____ _____ and _____ roads; encourage the sciences and arts by passing _____ laws and _____ laws; set up all federal _____ lower than the _____ _____; punish crimes at _____ or against _____ law; declare _____; raise and _____ the army, navy, and air force; call the states' _____ to enforce federal _____, end _____, or for defense against _____; organize and furnish weapons for the states' _____; govern the _____ of _____ and control all property in the states owned by the _____ _____; and pass laws to see that these _____ are carried out. This last clause is sometimes called the _____ _____ and gives Congress its _____ powers.

Some powers Congress may not have are: to take away the privilege of writs of _____ _____ except during times of _____ or _____; pass bills of _____ or _____ _____ _____ laws; tax _____; give to the ports of any one state any _____ over those of another, or tax goods shipped by _____ in the United States; draw money from the United States Treasury without an _____ of _____; or grant titles of _____.

Some powers the states may not have are: to make any separate _____; coin _____; use anything but _____ or _____ money in payment of debts; pass bills of _____, _____ _____ _____ laws, or laws that damage the _____ of contracts; or grant titles of _____. States must have the permission of Congress to tax _____ or _____; keep _____ or warships in time of peace; make agreements with other _____ or foreign _____; or fight a war unless actually _____ or in _____ danger.

WORDS YOU NEED TO KNOW

1. lay (raise; collect)
2. duty (tax on imports)
3. impost (tax on imports)
4. excise (tax on the manufacture, sale, or use of goods within a country)
5. uniform (the same)
6. commerce (trade; business)
7. naturalization (act of becoming a citizen of a country)
8. bankruptcy (act of turning over all one's holdings to those he owes to be legally free from debt, though his holdings are not equal in value to his debts)

9. standard (definite scale)
10. counterfeit (imitation; false)
11. patent (a license granted by the government giving inventors and discoverers the only rights to their works for a limited period of time)
12. copyright (a license granted by the government giving authors, artists, and musicians the only rights to their works for a limited period of time)
13. tribunal (court)
14. appropriation (amount set aside for a special purpose)
15. militia (state armed force; National Guard)
16. insurrection (rebellion)
17. purchase (buy)
18. authority (power)
19. magazine (storage place for ammunition)
20. arsenal (storage place for weapons)
21. elastic clause (power given to Congress to make laws to see that its other powers are carried out)
22. denied (not allowed; prohibited)
23. migration (movement from one place to another)
24. prohibit (forbid)
25. writ of *habeas corpus* (legal paper stating the right of a jailed person to be released if proper charges cannot be brought against him)
26. exceed (go beyond)
27. suspend (take away; end)
28. rebellion (war to overthrow the government)
29. invasion (crossing of a country's borders by enemy troops)
30. bill of attainder (a law that punishes a single individual and denies him the right to a trial)
31. *ex post facto* law (law making a crime of an act done before the time of making the law)
32. proportion (relation; ratio)
33. title of nobility (mark of rank raising a person above other citizens and sometimes above the law)
34. emolument (payment for service)
35. obligation (legal or moral duty)

36. compact (agreement; contract)
37. imminent (near; immediate)

WHERE TO LOOK

To find the names of the officers and members of Congress, get one of these books from your library:
1. *The World Almanac*
2. *United States Government Organization Manual*

ARTICLE II. THE EXECUTIVE
(law-enforcing) BRANCH
SECTION 1. The President and Vice-President

The President is the Chief Executive (person who sees that laws are enforced, or carried out). He and the Vice-President serve together for a four-year term. The Twenty-second Amendment limits the President to two terms.

The President and Vice-President are elected by electors (persons chosen to cast a state's votes for President and Vice-President). Each state has as many electors and electoral votes as it has senators and representatives in Congress. All electors in the United States make up what is called the electoral college. The "electoral college" never meets in a single group. Each state's electors meet in that state.

The manner in which electors are chosen is left up to the legislature of each state. Originally they were chosen by the members of the state legislature, but today they are elected by the people in every state. No one who holds any other United States office may be elected as an elector.

When the voters go to the polls (voting places), they vote for the electors nominated by the political party of their choice. This is done in the primary election (election held to elect candidates within a political party).

Candidates for President and Vice-President are not nominated (named to run for office) in primary elections, however. They are nominated by a national party convention (meeting) of party delegates (representatives) sent to the convention from all the states. The national conventions are held (in any cities the parties choose) sometime during the summer before the November elections.

Congressmen of both houses and electors, as well as various candidates for elected state and local offices, are nominated in primary elections.

The Constitution makes no mention of political parties, but by and large, the nominating, campaigning, and voting are controlled by our two major political parties, the Democratic party and the Republican party.

In the general election (regular election), the voter votes for the presidential and vice-presidential candidates of his choice by name, but in reality he is voting for the electors of his candidates' party.

The names of the candidates for President and Vice-President who are running together are placed on the same ballot (vote to be cast), and the voter must vote for both at once. This prevents the election of a President from one party and a Vice-President from another.

As a rule, all the electoral votes of a state go to the presidential and vice-presidential candidates who win a majority in that state. Only three states legally require their electors to vote for the candidates who win the majority vote, but it is a rare case indeed when an elector votes against the candidates of his party.

At first the electors voted for any two men, provided one of them lived in some state other than that of the electors. Both men were candidates for both offices of President and Vice-President. The electoral votes were then counted, signed, certified (declared true), sealed, and sent to the President of the Senate. All the electoral votes from all the states were counted in the presence of both houses of Congress. The candidate who received the highest number of votes above a majority was elected President, and the candidate with the second highest number was elected Vice-President. If two candidates had a majority and an equal number of votes, the House of Representatives elected one of them President. If no candidate had a majority, the House of Representatives elected the President from the five candidates with the most electoral votes. The voting in the House of Representatives was done by states, and each state—not each representative—had one vote. A quorum was two thirds of all the states, and to be elected President, a candidate had to receive a majority of all the states.

The Senate elected the Vice-President if two or more candidates had an equal number of electoral votes for second place.

The Twelfth Amendment changed this in 1804. Today, the electors in each state must say which candidate is the presidential candidate and which is the vice-presidential candidate. If, after the electoral votes are counted in the presence of both houses of Congress, no presidential candidate has a majority, the House of Representatives elects the President from among the three presidential candidates with the highest number of electoral votes. The manner in which this vote is taken in the House remains the same; each state has one vote, two thirds of the states make a quorum, and a majority of all the states is necessary to elect a President.

If a vice-presidential candidate does not get a majority of the electoral votes, the Senate elects the Vice-President from the two vice-presidential candidates with the highest number of electoral votes. Each Senator has one vote; a quorum is two thirds of all the senators; and it takes a majority of all the senators to elect a Vice-President.

Congress sets the date for voting for electors and the date electors vote for President and Vice-President. These dates are: the Tuesday after the first Monday in November of every fourth year for the election of electors; and the first Monday after the second Wednesday in December for the electors to vote for President and Vice-President. Both houses of Congress, sitting together, count the electoral votes on the sixth of January.

To be President or Vice-President, a person must meet the following qualifications:

1. Be a natural-born citizen.
2. Be at least thirty-five years old.
3. Have lived in the United States at least fourteen years.

The offices of President and Vice-President are the only ones, under the federal government, that a naturalized citizen cannot hold.

It is possible for a natural-born citizen to live away from this country for many years. To make sure our President is familiar with our way of life, he is required to have lived fourteen years in this country.

When for any reason (removal, resignation, or death), the President leaves his office, the Vice-President becomes President.

The Twenty-fifth Amendment gives the President the power to appoint a Vice-President if that office is open. A majority of both houses of Congress must agree to whomever he appoints.

This means that if a Vice-President becomes President, he can appoint someone to take his place as Vice-President.

Under ordinary circumstances this would always provide a Vice-President to replace the President in the event the President resigned, died, or was removed from office. But should it occur for any reason that both the offices of President and Vice-President become vacant at the same time, a law has been passed by Congress determining who will be next in line.

Next in line of presidential succession (following in the proper order) is the Speaker of the House; after him, the president pro tempore of the Senate; and after him, the President's Cabinet members in the order that their departments were established (set up). The Secretary of Health, Education, and Welfare, the Secretary of Housing and Urban Development, and the Secretary of Transportation are not included in the line of succession because their departments were not established until after the law of presidential succession had been passed by Congress.

The Vice-President becomes Acting President if the

President is unable to carry out his duties. This has never happened because no one had ever been able to decide just who or what determined when the President was unable to do his duties. (The Twenty-fifth Amendment now explains this.)

The President receives a salary of $200,000 a year, plus expense allowances amounting to $165,000 a year, the White House for his place of living, free medical care, cars, airplanes, ships, and trains for his use, and other benefits. His salary and $50,000 of his expense allowances are taxable. The President's salary may not be increased or lowered during his term of office, and he cannot accept any other payment from the United States or from any state while he is President.

The Vice-President receives a salary of $79,125 a year, plus $10,000 a year in expense allowances, all of which is taxable.

Before he may enter office, the President must take the following oath (sacred promise): "I do solemnly swear (or affirm) that I will faithfully execute [carry out] the office of president of the United States, and will to the best of my ability, preserve, protect and defend the constitution of the United States." This oath is usually given by the Chief Justice on January 20, the day of the President's inauguration (ceremony connected with entering office).

SECTION 2. Powers of the President

The powers of the President are:
1. Power of Commander in Chief of the armed forces of the United States and of the state militias when they are on active service with the United States armed forces.
2. Power to require, in writing, opinions from the principal (chief) officers in each of the executive departments. (The Constitution does not set up the President's Cabinet, or group of advisers, but this is the statement on which the idea for a Cabinet is based. The Cabinet has twelve members:

1. Secretary of State
2. Secretary of the Treasury
3. Secretary of Defense
4. Attorney General
5. Secretary of the Interior
6. Secretary of Agriculture
7. Secretary of Commerce
8. Secretary of Labor
9. Secretary of Health and Human Services
10. Secretary of Housing and Urban Development
11. Secretary of Transportation
12. Secretary of Energy
13. Secretary of Education

The Cabinet members are appointed by the President, with the consent of the Senate, for no definite term and receive $69,630 a year as salary.)

3. Power to grant reprieves (orders to delay or suspend the carrying out of court sentences) and pardons (orders to release persons convicted of crimes) to breakers of federal laws, but not to officials who have been removed by impeachment trials.

4. Power to make treaties with foreign countries, with the consent of two thirds of the Senate.

5. Power to appoint, with the Senate's consent, ambassadors (official representatives of the United States government in foreign countries), consuls (United States government officials who watch over United States commercial interests in foreign countries), judges of the Supreme Court, and all other officers of the United States government, which are established by law, and not otherwise provided for by the Constitution; but Congress may allow the appointment of inferior (lower in rank) officers by the President alone, by courts of law, or by heads of departments.

6. Power to make temporary appointments; if the Senate has adjourned, he may fill vacancies in government offices until the next session of the Senate ends, without the consent of the Senate.

SECTION 3. Duties of the President

Duties the President must carry out are:

1. He must from time to time (at the beginning of each session) inform Congress as to the "state of the union" (condition of the country), and ask that laws that he thinks are necessary and needed be passed.
2. He may convene (call back to session) either house or both houses of Congress if a national emergency (happening that needs to be acted upon at once) arises.
3. He may adjourn Congress if the two houses cannot reach an agreement as to when to adjourn (this has never happened).
4. He must receive ambassadors and other public ministers (representatives) from foreign nations.
5. He must see that the laws of the United States are carried out faithfully.
6. He must commission (make official by his signature) all the officers of the United States. About half of these officers are appointed through the United States Civil Service Commission.

SECTION 4. Impeachment

The President, Vice-President, and all civil (nonmilitary) officers of the United States may be impeached and removed from office if convicted of treason, bribery (payment for favors, breaking the trust of office), or other high crimes, or misdemeanors (crimes considered less serious than felonies). This does not include members of Congress. It was pointed out earlier that Congress does the impeaching: the House accuses; the Senate tries. A congressman is removed by being expelled by a two-thirds vote of his house.

CHECK YOURSELF
See if you can fill in the blanks.
Look back for any answer you do not know.

The executive branch includes the _____, the
_____, and the _____ _____. The President sees
that our laws are executed, or _____ _____.

Voters do not vote directly for President and Vice-
President. They vote for _____, who vote for them.
A state has as many _____ as it has _____ and
_____ combined. They make up what we call the
_____ _____. The _____ votes are counted and
certified in the states and are then sent to the _____
of the _____. They are then counted in the presence
of _____ _____ of Congress. If a presidential candidate does not get a _____ of _____ votes, the
House of Representatives elects a President from among
the _____ candidates with the most _____ votes. If
a vice-presidential candidate does not get a _____ of
_____ votes, the _____ elects a Vice-President from
the _____ with the most _____ votes.

The day electors are elected is the _____ after the
first _____ in _____ every _____ years. The day
the electors vote for President and Vice-President is the
first _____ after the _____ _____ in _____,
and the day these votes are counted by Congress is
_____ _____.

The President must be at least _____ years old, a
_____ citizen, and have lived in the United
States for _____ years. The Vice-President must meet
the same _____.

The President is followed in succession by the
_____, the _____ of the _____, the _____
_____ _____ of the _____, and his _____
_____ in the order their departments were _____.
The last _____ departments _____ are not in the
line of succession.

The President's salary is _____ dollars a year, plus

expense _____ and other benefits. The Vice-President's salary is _____ dollars a year.

The President and Vice-President serve _____ year terms of office, and the President is limited to _____ terms by the _____ Amendment to the Constitution.

The President takes an _____ of office, in which he _____ or _____ to carry out his _____ and defend the United States Constitution.

Among the powers and duties of the President are: _____ in _____ of the armed forces; to ask for _____ reports from the heads of executive _____; to grant _____ and _____ to breakers of federal laws, with the exception of _____ officials, who have been convicted; to make treaties with foreign countries, with the _____ of the Senate; to appoint _____, _____, _____ _____ _____, and other high officials, with the _____ of the Senate; to make _____ appointments if the Senate is not in session; to make a _____ of the _____ message to Congress at the beginning of each new session; to receive _____ from foreign countries; and to commission all federal _____.

A President may be impeached for _____, _____, other high crimes, or _____.

WORDS YOU NEED TO KNOW

1. executive (person who sees that acts are carried out properly; an enforcer)
2. Chief Executive (President of the United States)
3. elector (person elected by the people of a state to cast a vote for President and Vice-President)
4. electoral vote (votes cast by state electors to elect the President and Vice-President)
5. electoral college (all the electors in the United States)
6. polls (voting places)
7. primary election (election held before the general

election to nominate candidates within a political party to run in the general election)

8. nominate (name to run for office)
9. convention (meeting)
10. general election (any regular election to fill public offices)
11. certify (make official; declare true)
12. succession (following in proper order)
13. Cabinet (President's advisers, who head executive departments)
14. swear (promise; take oath)
15. oath (sacred promise)
16. affirm (promise on one's honor)
17. inauguration (ceremony connected with taking office)
18. principal (chief; first)
19. reprieve (order to delay or suspend the carrying out of a court sentence)
20. pardon (order to release a person convicted of a crime)
21. ambassador (official representative of one government to another)
22. consul (official who watches over commercial interests of one country in another)
23. inferior (lower in rank)
24. "state of the union" message (address made by the President to Congress at the beginning of each session recommending needed laws to improve the condition of the nation)
25. commission (give official recognition)
26. bribery (payment for favors that cause the breaking of the trust of office)
27. misdemeanors (crimes less serious than felonies; minor criminal acts)

WHERE TO LOOK

For more information about the President, Vice-President, the Cabinet, electoral college, election results, and names of executive officers, get the following books from your library:

1. *The World Almanac*
2. *United States Government Organization Manual*
3. *Facts about the Presidents*
4. *Pictorial History of American Presidents*

IN BRIEF

The executive department
I. The President and Vice-President
   A. Represent all the people of the United States
   B. Serve four-year terms
   C. Salaries
      1. President—$200,000 a year
      2. Vice-President—$79,125 a year
   D. Qualifications
      1. Must be at least thirty-five years old
      2. Must be a natural-born citizen
      3. Must have lived in the United States at least fourteen years
   E. Elected by electors, who are elected by the people in each state
II. The Cabinet
   A. Members in order of the establishment of their departments
      1. Secretary of State (1789)
      2. Secretary of the Treasury (1789)
      3. Secretary of Defense (originally War, 1789)
      4. Attorney General (1789)
      5. Secretary of the Interior (1849)
      6. Secretary of Agriculture (1889)
      7. Secretary of Commerce (1903)
      8. Secretary of Labor (1913)
      9. Secretary of Health and Human Services (1953, 1980)
      10. Secretary of Housing and Urban Development (1966)

11. Secretary of Transportation (1967)
12. Secretary of Energy (1977)
13. Secretary of Education (1980)
B. Serve no definite period
C. Salary—$69,630 a year
D. Appointed by the President with the consent of the Senate

ARTICLE III. THE JUDICIAL
(law-interpreting) BRANCH
SECTION 1. The Federal Courts

The judicial power (power to hear and judge cases) is vested in (given to and held by) the Supreme Court of the United States and such inferior courts (courts lower than the Supreme Court) as Congress may ordain (order) and establish (set up).

At the present time there are three regular federal courts (courts that hear criminal and civil cases):

1. The Supreme Court
2. The courts of appeals
3. The district courts

and four special federal courts (courts that hear only certain kinds of cases):

1. The Court of Claims
2. The Court of Customs and Patent Appeals
3. The Court of International Trade
4. The Tax Court

The judicial branch may be called upon to interpret (explain) a federal, state, or local law, and decide whether or not it is constitutional. No federal court ever declares a law unconstitutional (against what is said in the Constitution) unless someone breaks the law, and then defends himself in court, by saying the law takes away some constitutional right and should not be a law. He may, if necessary, appeal his case all the way to the Supreme Court before he receives a final decision.

Federal judges are appointed by the President, with the consent of the Senate, for a term of life. They may be impeached for poor behavior. They are paid for their services, and their salaries may not be lowered while they remain in office.

SECTION 2. Jurisdiction (power of judgment over certain cases) of the Federal Courts

The judicial power of the federal courts includes all cases of law—criminal cases (cases concerning lawbreakers), civil cases (cases concerning disputes or disagreements between parties), and cases of equity (cases concerning asking for court action to prevent some wrong or end some wrong being done) mentioned in the Constitution as well as:

1. Laws of the United States.
2. Treaties made by the United States.
3. Cases involving foreign representatives.
4. Cases of admiralty (crimes at sea) and maritime (ocean shipping) jurisdiction.
5. Controversies (disputes) in which the United States is involved.
6. Disputes between two or more states.
7. Disputes between citizens of different states.
8. Disputes in which citizens of the same state claim lands granted by different states.

At first, the federal courts also had the power to hear and try cases involving disputes between a state and citizens of another state and between a state and a foreign country. The Eleventh Amendment now gives this power to the state courts.

The Supreme Court has original jurisdiction (the power to try a case first) over cases that involve ambassadors, public ministers, and consuls; and cases in which a dispute between states is involved.

The Supreme Court has appellate jurisdiction (power to re-try a case already tried in a lower court) over all other cases mentioned in the Constitution. Congress may regulate and make exceptions to the Supreme Court's appellate jurisdiction.

The Supreme Court has appellate jurisdiction over a case only when one party (side) of the case is not satisfied with the decision (judgment, or ruling) made in the lower court and appeals to (asks for a new trial in) the higher court. An appeal may not be accepted if the Supreme Court feels there is no doubt as to the fairness of the decision in the lower court.

There are nine justices (judges) in the Supreme Court —one Chief (head) Justice and eight associate (co-operating) justices. They are appointed by the President with the consent of the Senate and serve life terms. (Federal judges are given their jobs for life, because it is felt that a judge who is secure in his job will be harder to bribe or corrupt in any way than one who is elected to a short term of office.)

The Chief Justice receives a salary of $96,800 a year, and the associate justices receive $93,000 a year. Both may receive disability or old-age retirement pensions.

All crimes tried in the federal courts are tried by jury (a group that decides the innocence or guilt of a person on trial). A petit jury (trial jury) usually has twelve members, who must give a unanimous vote to find an accused person guilty. The trials take place in the states where the crimes are committed, but if the crime does not take place within any state (crimes at sea, for example), Congress may decide where the trial will be held.

SECTION 3. *Treason*

Treason against the United States is defined as levying (making) war against the United States or giving aid and comfort (any help) to the enemies of the United States. To convict a person of treason, there must be two witnesses who actually saw the person commit the traitorous act, or the accused person must confess (admit) to it in a public court.

Congress decides how treason is punished. Conviction of treason cannot result in corruption of blood (make all members of the traitor's family and his descendants guilty); or forfeiture (loss of property as payment for a wrongdoing) except during the life of the person convicted of treason. This protects the traitor's family from unfair punishment.

CHECK YOURSELF
See if you can fill in the blanks.
Look back for any answer you do not know.

The judicial branch includes the _____ _____ and such _____ _____ as Congress sets up from time to time.

At the present time, there are three regular federal courts: the _____ _____, the _____ of _____, and the _____ _____; and three special federal courts: the _____ of _____, the _____ of _____ and _____ _____, and the _____ _____.

Federal judges are appointed by the _____ with the _____ of the Senate. They serve a _____ term but may be _____ for misconduct. Their salaries cannot be _____ while they remain in office.

The federal courts _____, or explain, the laws when required to do so. They may rule on _____, _____, or _____ laws.

The Supreme Court has both _____ and _____ jurisdiction.

There are _____ Supreme Court justices; one _____ Justice and _____ _____ justices.

All crimes tried in federal courts are tried by _____.

The Constitution defines treason as: making _____ against the United States; or helping the _____ of the United States. Unless there are _____ _____ who see a person commit an act of treason, or the person accused of treason _____, he cannot be convicted. The person guilty of treason is the only person punished. His _____ cannot be made guilty by _____ of _____; and _____ may not continue after the death of the traitor.

WORDS YOU NEED TO KNOW

1. judicial (pertaining to courts)
2. judicial branch (the United States system of courts)

3. interpret (explain)
4. inferior courts (courts lower than the Supreme Court)
5. jurisdiction (power to try a case)
6. original jurisdiction (power to try a case first)
7. appellate jurisdiction (power to re-try a case already tried in a lower court)
8. criminal case (court case concerned with lawbreakers)
9. civil case (court case concerning a disagreement between parties)
10. party (one side of a dispute—a person, a group, a company, etc.)
11. equity case (case concerning asking for court action to prevent a wrong or end a wrong being done)
12. controversy (dispute; disagreement)
13. decision (judgment; ruling)
14. appeal (request for new trial in a higher court)
15. jury (group selected to decide innocence or guilt of an accused person on trial)
16. confess (admit; tell)
17. corruption of blood (belief that the "bad blood" of a criminal flows in the veins of all members of his family)
18. forfeiture (loss of property as payment for a wrong act)
19. claims (demands made against)
20. appraisal (estimated worth; value placed upon)

WHERE TO LOOK

To learn the names of the Supreme Court justices get this book from your library:
The World Almanac

IN BRIEF

The federal judiciary
 I. Regular Courts
   A. Supreme Court
      1. Set up by the United States Constitution

      2. Has nine justices
        a. Chief Justice
        b. Eight associate justices
      3. Justices serve life terms
      4. Salaries
        a. Chief Justice—$96,800 a year
        b. Associate justices—$93,000 a year
      5. Has both original and appellate jurisdiction
   B. Courts of appeals
      1. Set up by Congress for purpose of relieving the Supreme Court of having to hear all appeals from the lower federal courts
      2. Have 84 judges—eleven courts
      3. Judges serve life terms
      4. Salaries—$74,300 a year
      5. Have appellate jurisdiction
   C. District courts
      1. Set up by Congress as trial courts
      2. Have 316 judges—eighty-eight courts
      3. Judges serve life terms
      4. Salaries—$70,300 a year
      5. Have original jurisdiction
II. Special courts
   A. Court of Claims
      1. Set up by Congress to decide if certain kinds of claims (demands) against the United States or branches of its government are true and if payment of these claims should be made
      2. Has five judges
      3. Judges serve life terms
      4. Salaries—$74,300 a year
      5. Has original jurisdiction; appellate jurisdiction over Indian Claims Commission
      6. Located in Washington, D. C.
   B. Court of Customs and Patent Appeals
      1. Set up by Congress to review decisions of the Customs Court and decisions of the United States Patent Office
      2. Has five judges
      3. Judges serve life terms
      4. Salaries—$74,300 a year

      5. Has appellate jurisdiction
      6. Located in Washington, D. C.
  C. Court of International Trade
      1. Set up by Congress to have jurisdiction over civil actions arising under tariff laws
      2. Has nine judges
      3. Judges serve life term
      4. Salaries—$70,300 a year
      5. Has original jurisdiction in controversies over value of merchandise, duties chargeable, and status of imports
      6. Located in New York, New York
  D. Tax Court
      1. Set up by Congress to have jurisdiction over cases involving over- or underpayment of taxes
      2. Has 16 judges
      3. Judges serve life terms
      4. Salaries—$70,300 a year
      5. Has original jurisdiction over cases involving income, gift, estate, and personal holding company surtaxes as determined by the IRS
      6. Located in Washington, D. C.

ARTICLE IV. DIRECTIONS FOR THE STATES
SECTION 1. State Laws, Records, and Court Decisions

Every state in the United States is required to recognize (respect) and give full credit to the laws, records, and court decisions of every other state. This prevents a person from escaping his lawful duties, or court action against him, simply by crossing a state line. Birth certificates, marriages, wills, deeds, and in most cases, divorces are recognized from state to state. Notice that this applies to civil law only. No state tries to enforce the criminal laws of any other state.

Congress may pass laws stating the manner in which these laws, records, and court decisions may be proved and what effects they may have upon the states.

SECTION 2. Rights of Citizens

A citizen of any state must receive, in all the other states, all the privileges (rights) and immunities (protections) that he has as a United States citizen. A person who moves from one state to another may not vote in the state to which he moves, however, until he lives there long enough to become a citizen of that state. In the meantime he may vote in national elections in the state from which he has come by using an absentee ballot (a vote sent through the mail by a person away from his state).

Any person charged in any state with treason, felony, or any other crime who escapes to another state may be returned to the state from which he escaped to stand trial or be sent back to prison if the governor of that state requests his return. The governor of the state to which he has escaped does not have to return him though, unless he chooses to do so. The return of an escaped fugitive (person wanted by the law) to one state by another is called extradition.

During the time slavery existed in this country, slaves who escaped from one state to another had to be returned to their masters.

SECTION 3. New States

New states may be admitted to the United States by Congress, but no new state can be made by dividing a state without the consent of Congress and of the state legislature of the state to be divided. No new state can be made by joining two or more states together or by joining together parts of two or more states without the consent of Congress and the consent of all the states' legislatures concerned.

Congress has the power to make rules and regulations for all territories (land regions owned by the United States) and other property belonging to the United States. The Constitution makes no statements meant to give false ideas in regard to lands claimed by the United States or by any particular state.

SECTION 4. *Guarantees Made to the States*

The United States guarantees (gives permanent assurance) that every state shall have a republican (representative) type of government, that it will protect each state against invasion, and if the legislature—or governor, when the legislature cannot be convened—requests it, protection against domestic violence (riots; mob action).

ARTICLE V. AMENDING THE CONSTITUTION

The Constitution is amended in two steps.
The amendment must be proposed by:
1. two thirds of both houses of Congress; *or*
2. special conventions called by Congress at the request of two thirds of the states' legislatures. (This has never been done.)

The amendment must be ratified by:
1. three fourths of the states' legislatures; *or*
2. special conventions in three fourths of the states.

Notice that only the states can ratify an amendment. Since the states gave their permission to set up a federal government under the Constitution in the first place, only they have the right to add to it or change it, but Congress may state which means of ratification is to be used. State conventions for ratification have been used only once—to ratify Amendment Twenty-one (repeal of federal prohibition).

No amendment could be made before 1808 that would affect the slave trade.

No amendment can be made to take away any state's equal representation in the Senate without the state's consent.

The procedure for amending the Constitution found in Article V is called formal amendment. In addition to formal amendment, we also have what is called informal amendment, which is actually not a means of amending the Constitution at all. But informal amendment is important because it includes all the developments made in the everyday experience of government under the Constitution. Some means and examples of informal amendment are:

1. Legislation—laws providing anything in government not specifically called for in the Constitution.
2. Executive action—the ways Presidents have carried out their powers.
3. Court decisions—interpretations of what is or is not constitutional.
4. Political party practices—the means of selecting party candidates to run for office.
5. Custom—time-approved actions taken by officers in our government that are not called for in the Constitution.

ARTICLE VI. RANKING OUR LAWS

All debts made by the United States under the Articles of Confederation were made valid (still in effect) against the United States under the Constitution.

The United States Constitution and United States laws and treaties are the supreme (highest) laws of the land. Any state constitution or any state law that conflicts with (differs from) the United States Constitution or United States laws or treaties cannot be enforced. State judges must uphold this in the state courts.

The laws of the United States ranked from the highest to the lowest are:

1. The United States Constitution
2. United States laws and treaties (equal in rank; whichever is most recent is in effect)
3. State constitutions
4. State laws
5. Local laws (county, township, city)

All legislative, executive, and judicial officers of the United States government and of the states' governments must take an oath to support the United States Constitution.

No person may be kept from holding office in the United States government because of his religious beliefs.

ARTICLE VII. RATIFICATION

The writers of the Constitution provided that conventions in nine of the states must ratify the Constitution before it could be considered ratified by the United States. (By June 21, 1788, nine states had ratified it.)

The Constitutional Convention accepted the Constitution, as written, by unanimous consent, and dated it September 17, 1787, the twelfth year of independence of the United States. The delegates then witnessed it with their signatures.

The Constitution was signed by George Washington, president and delegate from Virginia; John Langdon and Nicholas Gilman of New Hampshire; Nathaniel Gorham and Rufus King of Massachusetts; William Samuel Johnson and Roger Sherman of Connecticut; Alexander Hamilton of New York; William Livingston, David Brearley, William Paterson, and Jonathan Dayton of New Jersey; Benjamin Franklin, Thomas Mifflin, Robert Morris, George Clymer, Thomas Fitzsimons, Jared Ingersoll, James Wilson, and Gouverneur Morris of Pennsylvania; George Read, Gunning Bedford, Jr., John Dickinson, Richard Bassett, and Jacob Broom of Delaware; James M'Henry, Daniel of St. Thomas Jenifer, and Daniel Carroll of Maryland; John Blair and James Madison, Jr., of Virginia; William Blount, Richard Dobbs Spaight, and Hugh Williamson of North Carolina; John Rutledge, Charles Cotesworth Pinckney, Charles Pinckney, and Pierce Butler of South Carolina; William Few and Abraham Baldwin of Georgia; and attested (witnessed) by William Jackson, secretary.

CHECK YOURSELF
See if you can fill in the blanks.
Look back for any answer you do not know.

Every state must respect the _____, _____, and _____ _____ of every other state.

A citizen of one state who moves to another has all the _____ and _____ held by citizens of that state except that he may not _____ until he has lived there for a required period of time. The return of a fugitive by the governor of one state to the governor of another is called _____.

No state may be _____ to make a new state unless _____ and the _____ _____ give their consent, nor can _____ or more states or _____ of _____ or more states be combined to make a new state unless the _____ of the states concerned and _____ give their consent.

Congress regulates and makes rules for United States _____ and all other _____ that belong to the United States.

Congress guarantees the states a _____ form of government, protection from _____, and if requested, protection from _____ _____.

An amendment to the Constitution may be proposed by _____ _____ of both houses of Congress or by a special _____ set up by Congress at the request of _____ _____ of the _____ _____. An amendment may be ratified by _____ _____ of the _____ _____ or by special _____ in _____ _____ of the states.

No amendment may be made that would _____ _____ any state's right to have _____ _____ in the _____ without the state's consent.

The United States Constitution and United States _____ are always above _____ _____ and _____ _____. If a state law conflicts with a _____ law, the state law cannot be _____.

All _____, _____, and _____ officers of the United States and of the states must take an oath to _____ the _____ _____ _____.

No person may be kept from taking an office in the United States government because of his _____ beliefs.

WORDS YOU NEED TO KNOW

1. absentee ballot (official mail-in ballot)
2. fugitive (one who flees; one escaping from the law)
3. extradition (the return of a fugitive by one authority to another)
4. territory (land region belonging to a government)
5. guarantee (assure)
6. domestic violence (riots; mob action)
7. valid (in effect; acceptable)
8. conflict (differ; disagree)
9. attested (witnessed)
10. republican form of government (representative government)

IN BRIEF

Checks and balances
   I. Some checks on Congress and the Supreme Court made by the President
      A. May veto bills of Congress
      B. May call special sessions of Congress
      C. May adjourn Congress if the House and Senate cannot agree on an adjournment date
      D. May withhold information from Congress
      E. Appoints Supreme Court justices
  II. Some checks on the President and the Supreme Court made by Congress
      A. May propose amendments to the Constitution that affect offices of President and Supreme Court
      B. May impeach and try President or Supreme Court justices
      C. May override the President's veto by two-thirds vote of each house
      D. Controls all spending of money in the United States government

   E. Senate may refuse to give its consent to an appointment to the Supreme Court
   F. Senate may refuse to give its consent to any other appointments or treaties made by the President
III. Some checks on the President and Congress made by the Supreme Court
   A. May declare laws, passed by Congress and signed by the President, unconstitutional
   B. May bring suits or issue court orders against public officers

PART III:

The Bill of Rights

The Constitution was sent to the states for ratification in 1787. People soon began to notice that it did not list many of the personal liberties (individual rights) they had come to believe were theirs. They wanted these rights written into the Constitution. In fact, a number of states, before ratifying, made it known that they expected a "Bill of Rights" to be added to the Constitution. Twelve amendments, containing the rights to be held by the people of the United States, were drawn up, and of these, ten were ratified and added to the Constitution in 1791.

The amendments are called "Articles of Amendment" by the Constitution, but we usually refer to them by number and the word "Amendment."

AMENDMENT 1. FIVE FREEDOMS

Congress cannot pass any law making any religion the religion of the United States, or take away the freedom to worship as one pleases. Congress cannot take away or restrict freedom of speech or freedom of the press. Citizens may protect themselves against damaging insults spoken or written about them by civil lawsuits, and no one may advocate (call for) the overthrow of the government by war. Congress may not take away the right

74

of peaceful assembly (gathering of people). Riots or mobs may be broken up, since they are not peaceful. The right of petitioning the government for any redress (correction) wanted made by it, or any grievance (complaint) made against it, may not be suspended.

AMENDMENT 2. RIGHT TO BEAR ARMS

For their protection and for purposes of having a well-trained militia the people of the states may keep and bear (own) arms (weapons), but the federal government or the state governments may pass laws against owning certain weapons and the way others may be used.

AMENDMENT 3. QUARTERING SOLDIERS

No civilian may be forced to quarter (give room and board to) soldiers except in time of war, and then only if Congress passes such a law. During the British rule, many people had been forced to do this, and they wanted to be sure their own government would not make this requirement of them.

AMENDMENT 4. UNREASONABLE SEARCHES AND SEIZURES

The right of the people to be secure (safe) from unreasonable searches or seizures (arrests or taking of belongings) of themselves, their houses, their papers and effects (other personal property) cannot be violated. Warrants (written court orders) for any of these purposes must be issued with good cause, sworn to by an oath, and must describe, in detail, the place to be searched and the persons or things to be seized. This protects persons from "writs of assistance" (general warrants allowing any search or seizure anytime anyplace) such as were used by the British.

AMENDMENT 5. PROTECTION FOR A PERSON ACCUSED OF A CRIME

Any person accused of a capital (serious) or infamous (horrible) crime, except a person on active duty with the military forces during time of war or public danger, must be indicted (charged and held for trial) by a grand jury (twelve to twenty-three persons selected to decide if there is enough evidence or information against the accused to hold a trial).

No one may be placed in double jeopardy (tried again for a crime for which he has already been tried and found innocent). If the crime breaks both a state and a federal law, the accused person may be tried in a state court after having been tried in a federal court.

No person can be forced to testify (speak) against himself.

No person may lose his life (be executed), liberty (be jailed), or property (be fined), except by due process of law (fair legal practices followed by the courts and based upon fair laws). The Fourteenth Amendment places this same restriction on the state courts.

No private property may be taken for public (government) use unless the owner is given fair compensation (payment) for it. If a person's property is needed for the good of all the people, he must sell it. One person cannot stand in the way of the progress of all the people.

AMENDMENT 6. RIGHTS OF A PERSON ACCUSED OF A CRIME

When prosecuted (brought to trial) for a crime, an accused person has these rights:

1. Right to a speedy (as soon as possible) and public (in front of people, to see it is fair) trial.
2. Right to an impartial (open-minded) jury selected from the state and judicial district where the crime was committed.
3. Right to hear charges made against him.
4. Right to hear witnesses against him.

5. Right to have witnesses in his favor, by means of subpoena (court order forcing witness to appear), if necessary.
6. Right to have assistance of counsel (a lawyer for his defense). If he is unable to pay a lawyer, the court must provide him one.

AMENDMENT 7. CIVIL LAW

In cases of common law (civil law), when the value of the object under dispute is more than twenty dollars, the parties in the dispute may ask for a jury trial. The jury's verdict (decision) is binding, but the case may be appealed to a higher court. This applies only to federal courts.

AMENDMENT 8. BAIL, FINES; CRUEL OR UNUSUAL PUNISHMENT

Unreasonably high bail (sum of money put up by an arrested person to insure his return, in order that he may be released until the time of his trial) must not be required, nor unreasonably high fines be imposed (charged), nor cruel and unusual punishments (torture or branding, for example) be inflicted (carried out as punishment).

Bail is usually set according to the seriousness of the crime, and for a serious crime may seem unreasonably high, but if bail were set too low, accused persons might be tempted to forfeit their bail and not return for trial. Bail may not be put up by persons considered too dangerous to be given their freedom until the time of their trial.

Death, as a punishment for a crime, is not considered cruel or unusual as long as there is no long physical suffering involved.

AMENDMENT 9. RIGHTS NOT LISTED

The enumeration (listing by number) of certain rights in the Constitution does not mean these are the only rights the people have. To list all the many rights the people of the United States simply take for granted would be impossible, but every citizen should be aware that he has these rights in order to protect them.

AMENDMENT 10. POWERS OF THE STATES AND PEOPLE

Any powers that are not the exclusive powers of the United States government, or that are not specifically denied the states' governments by the Constitution, are the powers of the states, or of the people. Some examples of state powers are: taxing; passing laws concerning education, marriage, divorce, contracts, inheritances, and corporations; setting up state courts; and regulating health, morals, safety, and public welfare.

CHECK YOURSELF
See if you can fill in the blanks.
Look back for any answer you do not know.

Amendment 1 guarantees freedom of _____, _____, _____, _____, and _____.

Amendment 2 gives the right to _____ _____ for the purpose of having well-trained _____.

Amendment 3 forbids the government to _____ _____ in private homes except during time of _____.

Amendment 4 forbids the _____ and _____ of a person or his property without a _____.

Amendment 5 says that no person may be tried in a federal court for a serious crime unless he is _____ by a _____ _____. Persons on active military service, during time of war, are excluded from this right.

No person may be placed in _____ _____.

No person may be forced to _____ against himself.

No person may be _____, _____, or _____ except by _____ _____ of law.

Private property may not be taken for _____ use unless the owner is paid a _____ _____ for it.

Amendment 6 provides that an accused person must be tried _____ and in _____. He has the right to a _____. He must hear _____ made against him and _____ who testify against him. He may have _____ subpoenaed to speak for him. He has the right to a _____, and if he cannot afford one, the _____ must provide one.

Amendment 7 states that if more than _____ dollars is involved in a civil suit, the disputing parties may have a _____ trial.

Amendment 8 says that no _____ high bail or _____ may be imposed and that no _____ or _____ punishments, such as _____ or _____, may be inflicted upon a person.

Amendment 9 informs the people that they have too many _____ to list them all in the Constitution, but these _____ are theirs and cannot be taken away.

Amendment 10 gives to the _____ and the _____ all powers not listed as _____ powers of the United States, or not specifically _____ the states.

WORDS YOU NEED TO KNOW

1. personal liberties (individual rights)
2. advocate (call for; speak or write in favor of)
3. assembly (gathering of people)
4. redress (correction)
5. grievance (complaint)
6. quarter (supply room and board for)
7. seizure (arrests or confiscations; taking of one's belongings)
8. effects (personal property)
9. warrant (written court order allowing the arrest,

search, and seizure of certain persons or certain property)

10. writs of assistance (general search warrants)
11. indict (charge with a crime and hold for trial)
12. grand jury (twelve to twenty-three persons selected to decide if evidence against an accused person is sufficient for holding a trial; indictment jury)
13. evidence (information; facts)
14. double jeopardy (being tried again for a crime already found not guilty of)
15. testify (speak; bear witness)
16. compensation (payment)
17. prosecute (accuse and attempt to prove guilty)
18. impartial (open-minded; not prejudiced)
19. verdict (decision; ruling)
20. bail (a sum of money put up by an arrested person to insure his return, in order to be released until the time of his trial)
21. enumeration (number; count)
22. counsel (lawyer; attorney)
23. subpoena (court order forcing a witness to appear in court)

WHERE TO LOOK

For more information about the Bill of Rights, get this book from your library:
The Living Bill of Rights by W. O. Douglas

PART IV:

Amendments Since the Bill of Rights

AMENDMENT 11 (1798). SUITS AGAINST THE STATES

No civil suit or equity suit brought against a state by citizens of another state or by citizens or subjects of any foreign country may be tried in the federal courts. These suits must be tried in the courts of that state. This changes Article III, Section 2.

AMENDMENT 12 (1804). ELECTING THE PRESIDENT AND VICE-PRESIDENT

The electors meet in their states and vote by ballot for both President and Vice-President, naming which candidate is the presidential candidate and which is the vice-presidential candidate. A separate list is made naming each candidate for each office and giving the number of votes received by each. These lists are signed by the electors, sealed, certified, and sent to Washington, D. C., addressed to the President of the Senate.

If no presidential candidate gets a majority of the electoral vote, the House of Representatives elects a President, by ballot, from the three candidates with the most electoral votes. A quorum in the House for this purpose is one or more representatives from two thirds of the states. The vote is taken by state and each state has one vote. A majority vote is necessary to elect a President.

If the House does not elect a President before the next January 20 (changed from March 4 by the Twentieth Amendment), the person elected Vice-President acts as President, just as he would in case of the death or any other constitutional disability of the President.

If no vice-presidential candidate gets a majority of electoral votes, the Senate elects a Vice-President from the two candidates with the most electoral votes. A quorum in the Senate for this purpose is two thirds of the senators, and a majority vote is necessary to elect a Vice-President.

No person ineligible (unable to meet the qualifications) for President may be elected Vice-President.

This changes Article II, Section 1 in part.

Today, for all practical purposes, casting the electoral vote is just a formality. With our modern voting machines, computers, radio, television, and news services, we are able to know who was elected President and Vice-President within a few hours after the election. Congress does not count the electoral vote until January, but we usually know the outcome as early as the first or second week in November.

AMENDMENT 13 (1865). SLAVERY ENDED

SECTION 1. Neither slavery nor involuntary servitude (work done against one's will), except as punishment for having been convicted of a crime, is allowed in the United States or any of its territories or possessions.

SECTION 2. Congress has the power to enforce this article by appropriate (necessary) legislation (laws). Constitutional powers of this sort are called enabling acts because they enable Congress to pass laws, seeing that the amendment is carried out.

AMENDMENT 14 (1868). CITIZENS' RIGHTS

SECTION 1. Any person born or naturalized in the United States and governed by it is a citizen of the United States and of the state in which he resides (lives).

No state can make laws that abridge (take away or restrict) any right, privilege, or protection of citizens of the United States; nor pass laws that may cost a person his life, imprison him, or fine him, unless he has been found guilty of a crime in a court of law by due process of law (following fair legal practices based upon fair laws).

No state may deny any person, under its government, equal protection of the law.

SECTION 2. Representatives to Congress are elected in each state according to that state's population. If any state takes away the right to vote for: (1) electors for President and Vice-President of the United States, (2) United States senators and representatives, or (3) any state executive, legislative, or judicial officers from any males of that state, who are: (a) twenty-one years of age, (b) citizens of the United States, and (c) have not been convicted of a crime or rebellion against the United States, the number of representatives for that state may be reduced in proportion to those persons not allowed to vote in that state.

This was to protect the Blacks' right to vote in the Southern states after the Civil War. It has never been enforced. It says the rights of male citizens to vote because women, at this time, did not have the right to vote.

SECTION 3. No person could be: (1) a United States senator or representative, (2) an elector for President and Vice-President, (3) a military or civilian officer of the United States, or (4) a state officer, if he had ever taken the oath to support the Constitution when elected as: (1) a United States senator or representative, (2) any other United States officer, or (3) a member of a state legislature, (4) a member of the state judiciary (courts), or (5) a state executive officer, and then had fought against the United States or given help to the Confederacy (Southern states that attempted to secede —withdraw—from the Union) during the Civil War.

Congress was given the power to do away with this section by a two-thirds vote, and did so in 1898.

SECTION 4. The United States promised to pay all the lawful debts it had made during the Civil War, including pensions and bounties (rewards) to persons who earned them fighting for the United States in the Civil War; but neither the United States nor any state was allowed to pay debts owed by the Confederacy, and no payment could be made for emancipated (freed) slaves. All debts, obligations, and claims against the Confederacy and in regard to freed slaves were considered illegal and void (not payable).

SECTION 5. Congress was given the power to enforce this amendment by appropriate legislation.

AMENDMENT 15 (1870). VOTING RIGHTS OF BLACKS

SECTION 1. The right of citizens of the United States to vote cannot be taken away because of a person's race, color, or previous condition of servitude (having been a slave).

SECTION 2. Congress has the power to enforce this amendment by appropriate legislation.

AMENDMENT 16 (1913). INCOME TAX

Congress has the power to lay and collect taxes on income (money earned by individuals or businesses) without respect to a state's population or census figures.

The income tax is collected yearly on a percentage

basis. The higher the earnings, the higher the percentage collected from them.

This changes Article I, Section 2.

AMENDMENT 17 (1913). ELECTION OF SENATORS

The Senate of the United States is composed (made up) of two senators from each state, who are elected by the people of the state they represent. Each senator serves a six-year term and has one vote in the Senate.

To vote for the senators from his state, a person must meet the same qualifications in his state for voting for the largest house in the state legislature.

When a state has a vacancy in the Senate, the governor of that state may make a temporary appointment to fill the vacancy if he has the permission of the state legislature to do so, or a special election may be called, giving the people of the state the opportunity to fill the vacancy.

The election or term of office of any senator who was chosen before the time this amendment went into effect was not affected by it.

This changes Article I, Section 3.

AMENDMENT 18 (1919). PROHIBITION OF INTOXICATING LIQUORS

SECTION 1. One year after the ratification of this amendment, the manufacture, sale, or transportation of intoxicating liquors (alcoholic drinks) within, into, or out of the United States or any territory governed by the United States was prohibited (forbidden and made against the law).

SECTION 2. Congress and the states' legislatures were given concurrent power (power held by both) to enforce this amendment by appropriate legislation.

SECTION 3. The states were given a period of seven years to ratify this amendment. After that time it could not have been adopted.

This amendment was repealed (canceled) in 1933 by the Twenty-first Amendment.

AMENDMENT 19 (1920). RIGHT TO VOTE FOR WOMEN

The right of the citizens of the United States to vote cannot be taken away or restricted because of a person's sex. This means women, since at the time men already had the right to vote.

Congress has the power to enforce this amendment by appropriate legislation.

Before this amendment was ratified, whether or not to let women vote was left up to the states. Nine states had permitted it.

AMENDMENT 20 (1933). EXECUTIVE AND LEGISLATIVE TERMS OF OFFICE

SECTION 1. The terms of the President and the Vice-President end at noon on January 20, and the terms of senators and representatives end at noon on January 3, of the year such terms ordinarily end. The terms of their successors (persons who hold office for the coming term) begin at the time these terms end.

This shortened the time between the election and the inauguration of the President by nearly two months.

SECTION 2. Congress must meet at least once a year. The first day of meeting begins at noon on January 3. Congress may set a new date for the first day of session if it chooses to do so.

This changes Article I, Section 4 in part. It prevents defeated congressmen from remaining in office for over a year before the newly elected ones are seated. Congressmen are elected in even-numbered years and attend their first session in odd-numbered years. Under the old system, a congressman was elected in November in one year but did not take his seat until December of the next.

SECTION 3. If, at the time fixed for the beginning of the term of President, the President-elect (person elected President for the coming term) has died, the Vice-President-elect becomes President.

If a President has not been elected, or if the President-elect, for some reason, cannot qualify for the office by the time the term begins, the Vice-President-elect acts as President until such time as a qualified President can be elected.

If neither the President-elect nor the Vice-President-elect can qualify for their offices, Congress may, by law, decide who shall act as President or the manner in which an acting President shall be selected. The Acting President shall serve until a qualified President or Vice-President is elected. None of these things has ever happened.

SECTION 4. If no presidential candidate has a majority of electoral votes, and the House of Representatives must elect a President, Congress may decide, by law, what is to be done if one or more of the candidates among the three with the most electoral votes should die before the House has elected a President. Congress may, by law, make the same decision in the case of the death of either, or both, vice-presidential candidates, when the Senate must elect a Vice-President.

Congress has never taken any action on this.

SECTION 5. Sections 1 and 2 took effect on the October 15 following the ratification of this amendment.

SECTION 6. The states' legislatures were given seven years to ratify this amendment. After that time it could not have been adopted.

AMENDMENT 21 (1933). REPEAL OF "PROHIBITION"

SECTION 1. The Eighteenth Amendment is repealed (done away with).

SECTION 2. Transportation or importation of intoxicating liquors, for delivery or use, into any states, territories, or possessions that have laws against the manufacture, transportation, or sale of alcoholic drinks is prohibited.

It is now the decision of each state as to whether to have "prohibition" or not, but the federal government makes it a crime to transport intoxicating liquors across the state line of any state that has "prohibition" laws. No state now has "prohibition," but individual counties within states have it.

SECTION 3. The states were given a period of seven years to ratify this amendment by conventions held in the states. After that time this amendment could not have been adopted.

This is the only amendment in which Congress calls for ratification by conventions. It was felt that conventions in the states would be more likely to ratify than the states' legislatures.

AMENDMENT 22 (1951). PRESIDENT'S TERM IS RESTRICTED

No person may be elected to the office of President more than twice.

Any person who has held the office of President, or acted as President for *more* than two years of a term to which some other person was elected, may be elected President only once.

Any person who has held the office of President, or acted as President for *less* than two years of a term to which some other person was elected, may be elected President twice.

This amendment did not apply to the President in office when it was proposed (Harry S Truman) and was not meant to prevent any person holding the office of President, or acting as President, from finishing his term of office when it was adopted.

AMENDMENT 23 (1961). RIGHT TO VOTE IN THE DISTRICT OF COLUMBIA

SECTION 1. The District of Columbia may appoint, in such manner as Congress directs, as many electors for President and Vice-President as it would have senators and representatives if it were a state, but it may not have more electors than the state with the least population. It may have three electors at the present time.

The electors of the District of Columbia are in addition to those of the states. The states do not lose any of their electors, but electors of the District of Columbia are considered, for the purposes of election of President and Vice-President, to be appointed by a state. They meet in the District of Columbia and perform the duties required of electors by the Twelfth Amendment.

SECTION 2. Congress has the power to enforce this amendment by appropriate legislation.

AMENDMENT 24 (1964). POLL TAX PROHIBITED

SECTION 1. No citizen can be denied his right to vote in any primary or other election for President or Vice-President, for electors for President or Vice-President, or for senators or representatives in Congress because he has not paid a poll tax or any other tax.

SECTION 2. Congress has the power to enforce this amendment by appropriate legislation.

AMENDMENT 25 (1967). PRESIDENTIAL SUCCESSION

SECTION 1. If the President is removed from office or dies or resigns, the Vice-President becomes President.

SECTION 2. If there is a vacancy in the office of the Vice-President (if the Vice-President has become President or if he has been removed from office or died or resigned), the President nominates (names) a Vice-President who takes office after both houses of Congress have confirmed (approved) him by a majority vote.

SECTION 3. If the President informs the president pro tempore of the Senate and the Speaker of the House of Representatives, in writing, that he is unable to carry out the powers and duties of his office, the Vice-President becomes Acting President until the President informs the president pro tempore and the Speaker of the House, in writing, that he is once again able to carry out the powers and duties of his office.

SECTION 4. If the Vice-President and a majority of the President's Cabinet (or some other group Congress may decide upon by law) inform the president pro tempore and the Speaker of the House, in writing, that the President is unable to carry out the powers and duties of his office, the Vice-President immediately becomes Acting President.

The President may resume (take back) his office when he informs the president pro tempore and the Speaker of the House, in writing, that he is able to carry out the powers and duties of his office, unless, within four days, the Vice-President and a majority of the President's Cabinet (or some other group Congress may decide upon by law) inform the president pro tempore and the Speaker of the House, in writing, that the President is still unable to carry out the powers and duties of his office. In the event this happens Congress must decide whether or not the President is capable. Should

Congress not be in session at the time, it must assemble within forty-eight hours. Congress must make a decision within twenty-one days (or twenty-one days after it has been called to session). If Congress decides, by a two-thirds vote of both houses, that the President is unable to carry out the powers and duties of his office, the Vice-President will continue as Acting President.

A wound from an attempted assassination, prolonged physical illness, and mental disability are three examples of why the President would be unable to carry out the powers and duties of his office.

AMENDMENT 26 (1971). VOTING AGE LOWERED

SECTION 1.　Citizens of the United States eighteen years or older may not be denied the right to vote by the United States or any state on account of age.

SECTION 2.　Congress has the power to enforce this amendment by appropriate legislation.

CHECK YOURSELF
See if you can fill in the blanks.
Look back for any answer you do not know.

Amendment 11 says that no _____ court may try a case in which a state is being sued by _____ of another _____; or_____ or _____ of a _____ _____.

Amendment 12 changes Article II, Section 1, by requiring electors to vote for _____ and _____ by name and office and to list the _____ of votes for each _____ for either office. The electoral votes are signed, sealed, _____, and sent to _____, addressed to the _____ of the _____. They are counted in the presence of both _____ of _____.

If no presidential candidate gets a _____ of _____ votes, the House elects a President from the _____ candidates with the most _____ votes. If no vice-presidential candidate has a _____ of _____ votes, the Senate elects a Vice-President from the _____ candidates with the most _____ votes.

Amendment 13 forbids _____. No person may be made to _____ against his will.

A number of amendments have _____ _____ that give Congress the power to enforce them.

Amendment 14 says that any person _____ or _____ in the United States is a _____ of the United States and of the _____ where he lives. No state may make or enforce any laws that take away the _____ or _____ of any citizen. No state may take a person's _____, _____, or _____ except by due process of _____.

If a state takes away the right to vote of some citizens, the number of _____ it has in _____ will be reduced in _____ to those who are not allowed to vote.

Amendment 15 says that the right to _____ cannot be denied a citizen because of his _____ or _____.

Amendment 16 sets up the federal _____ _____.

Amendment 17 gives the _____ of the states the right to elect _____. A vacancy in the Senate may be filled by the _____ of the state in which the vacancy occurs by a _____ _____ or by calling a _____ _____.

Amendment 18 prohibits the _____, _____, and _____ of _____ _____.

Amendment 19 gives _____ the right to vote.

Amendment 20 says that the terms of office for President and Vice-President begin and end at _____ on _____ _____. The terms of office for congressmen begin and end at _____ on _____ _____.

If a President-elect dies before he can take office, the _____ becomes President. If no President is elected by the time the President is to take office, or if the President-elect does not _____, the _____ acts as President until a President is elected. If neither the President-elect nor the Vice-President-elect qualifies, Congress may decide _____ will act as President or how an acting President will be _____.

Amendment 21 repeals _____ but allows each state to have _____ laws of its own.

Amendment 22 says that no person may be elected _____ for more than _____ _____. If a person serves as, or acts as, _____ for more than _____ years of a term to which someone else was elected, he may serve only _____ term. If a person serves or acts as _____ for less than _____ years of a term to which someone else was elected, he may serve _____ terms.

This amendment did not apply to President _____.

Amendment 23 gives the people of the _____ of _____ the right to vote for _____ for President and Vice-President. The _____ of _____ may not have more _____ than the state with the least number of _____, so it has _____.

Amendment 24 forbids states to require voters to pay a _____ _____ to vote in federal elections.

Amendment 25 says that when the President is _____ from office or has _____ or _____, the _____ becomes President.

The President _____ a Vice-President when that office has a _____, but Congress must _____ his choice with a _____ vote of both houses.

The President may temporarily remove himself from office by informing the _____ _____ _____ and the _____ _____ _____ _____, in writing, that he is unable to carry out the _____ and _____ of his office. The Vice-President becomes _____ _____ until the President is able to return.

The Vice-President and a _____ of the President's Cabinet can inform the _____ _____ _____ and the _____ of the _____, in writing, that the President is unable to carry out the _____ and _____ of his office, and the Vice-President becomes _____ _____. When the President feels he is able to resume his office, he may do so by informing, in writing, the same officers of Congress unless, within _____ days, the Vice-President and a _____ of the President's Cabinet inform the same officers of Congress, in writing, that he is unable to do so. Congress must then _____.

If Congress is not in session, it must meet within
_____ _____ and reach a decision within _____
_____ by a _____ vote of both houses.

Amendment 26 lowered the voting age to _____.

WORDS YOU NEED TO KNOW

1. ineligible (unable to meet certain qualifications for membership)
2. involuntary servitude (work done against one's will)
3. appropriate (necessary; needed)
4. legislation (laws)
5. abridge (restrict; take away)
6. Confederacy (Southern states that attempted to secede from the United States)
7. secede (withdraw)
8. emancipate (set free)
9. bounty (reward)
10. void (expired; no longer existing)
11. income tax (tax paid on earnings)
12. intoxicating liquors (alcoholic drinks)
13. repeal (cancel; end)
14. suffrage (right to vote)
15. successor (person who follows a preceding office-holder in his office)
16. poll tax (voting tax collected to pay cost of holding an election, and in some cases, to prevent certain citizens, who cannot afford to pay, from voting)
17. confirm (approve)

PART V:

The Constitution of the United States

Are You Ready?

The Constitution of the United States follows. If you have read this simplified, explained text carefully and studied the vocabulary, you should be able to understand the Constitution as it was originally written. Try, and see.

The Constitution of the United States of America

We the people of the United States, in order to form a more perfect union, establish justice, insure domestic tranquility, provide for the common defense, promote the general welfare, and secure the blessings of liberty to ourselves and our posterity, do ordain and establish this Constitution for the United States of America.

ARTICLE I.

SECTION 1. All legislative powers herein granted shall be vested in a Congress of the United States, which shall consist of a Senate and House of Representatives.

SECTION 2. The House of Representatives shall be composed of members chosen every second year by the people of the several states, and the electors in each state shall have the qualifications requisite for electors of the most numerous branch of the state legislature.

No person shall be a representative who shall not have attained to the age of 25 years, and been seven years a citizen of the United States, and who shall not, when elected, be an inhabitant of that state in which he shall be chosen.

Representatives and direct taxes shall be apportioned among the several states which may be included within this union, according to their respective numbers, which shall be determined by adding to the whole number of free persons, including those bound to service for a term of years, and excluding Indians not taxed, three-fifths of all other persons. The actual enumeration shall be made within three years after the first meeting of the Congress of the United States, and within every subsequent term of ten years, in such manner as they shall by law direct. The number of representatives shall not exceed one for every 30,000, but each state shall have at least one representative; and until such enumeration shall be made, the state of New Hampshire shall be entitled to choose three, Massachusetts eight, Rhode Island and Providence Plantations one, Connecticut five, New York six, New Jersey four, Pennsylvania eight, Delaware one, Maryland six, Virginia ten, North Carolina five, South Carolina five, and Georgia three.

When vacancies happen in the representation from any state, the executive authority thereof shall issue writs of election to fill such vacancies.

The House of Representatives shall choose their

speaker and other officers; and shall have the sole power of impeachment.

SECTION 3. The Senate of the United States shall be composed of two senators from each state, chosen by the legislature thereof, for six years; and each senator shall have one vote.

Immediately after they shall be assembled in consequence of the first election, they shall be divided as equally as may be into three classes. The seats of the senators of the first class shall be vacated at the expiration of the second year, of the second class at the expiration of the fourth year, and of the third class at the expiration of the sixth year, so that one-third may be chosen every second year; and if vacancies happen by resignation, or otherwise, during the recess of the legislature of any state, the executive thereof may make temporary appointments until the next meeting of the legislature, which shall then fill such vacancies.

No person shall be a senator who shall not have attained to the age of 30 years, and been nine years a citizen of the United States, and who shall not, when elected, be an inhabitant of that state for which he shall be chosen.

The vice-president of the United States shall be president of the Senate, but shall have no vote, unless they be equally divided.

The Senate shall choose their other officers, and also a president pro tempore, in the absence of the vice-president, or when he shall exercise the office of president of the United States.

The Senate shall have the sole power to try all impeachments. When sitting for that purpose, they shall be on oath or affirmation. When the president of the United States is tried, the chief justice shall preside: And no person shall be convicted without the concurrence of two-thirds of the members present.

Judgment in cases of impeachment shall not extend

further than to removal from office, and disqualification to hold and enjoy any office of honour, trust or profit under the United States; but the party convicted shall nevertheless be liable and subject to indictment, trial, judgment and punishment, according to law.

SECTION 4. The times, places and manner of holding elections, for senators and representatives, shall be prescribed in each state by the legislature thereof; but Congress may at any time by law make or alter such regulations, except as to the places of choosing senators.

The Congress shall assemble at least once in every year, and such meeting shall be on the first Monday in December, unless they shall by law appoint a different day.

SECTION 5. Each house shall be the judge of the elections, returns and qualifications of its own members, and a majority of each shall constitute a quorum to do business; but a smaller number may adjourn from day to day, and may be authorized to compel the attendance of absent members, in such manner, and under such penalties as each house may provide.

Each house may determine the rules of its proceedings, punish its members for disorderly behaviour, and, with the concurrence of two-thirds, expel a member.

Each house shall keep a journal of its proceedings, and from time to time publish the same, excepting such parts as may in their judgment require secrecy; and the yeas and nays of the members of either house on any question shall, at the desire of one-fifth of those present, be entered on the journal.

Neither house, during the session of Congress, shall, without the consent of the other, adjourn for more than three days, nor to any other place than that in which the two houses shall be sitting.

SECTION 6. The senators and representatives shall receive a compensation for their services, to be ascertained by law, and paid out of the treasury of the United

States. They shall in all cases, except treason, felony and breach of the peace, be privileged from arrest during their attendance at the session of their respective houses, and in going to and returning from the same; and for any speech or debate in either house, they shall not be questioned in any other place.

No senator or representative shall, during the time for which he was elected, be appointed to any civil office under the authority of the United States, which shall have been created, or the emoluments whereof shall have been increased during such time; and no person holding any office under the United States, shall be a member of either house during his continuance in office.

SECTION 7. All bills for raising revenue shall originate in the House of Representatives; but the Senate may propose or concur with amendments as on other bills.

Every bill which shall have passed the House of Representatives and the Senate, shall, before it becomes a law, be presented to the president of the United States; if he approve, he shall sign it, but if not, he shall return it, with his objections, to that house in which it shall have originated, who shall enter the objections at large on their journal, and proceed to reconsider it. If after such reconsideration, two-thirds of that house shall agree to pass the bill, it shall be sent, together with the objections, to the other house, by which it shall likewise be reconsidered, and if approved by two-thirds of that house, it shall become a law. But in all such cases the votes of both houses shall be determined by yeas and nays, and the names of the persons voting for and against the bill shall be entered on the journal of each house respectively. If any bill shall not be returned by the president within ten days, (Sundays excepted) after it shall have been presented to him, the same shall be a law, in like manner as if he had signed it, unless the Congress by their adjournment prevent its return, in which case it shall not be a law.

Every order, resolution, or vote to which the concurrence of the Senate and House of Representatives may be necessary (except on a question of adjournment) shall be presented to the president of the United States; and before the same shall take effect, shall be approved by him, or, being disapproved by him, shall be re-passed by two-thirds of the Senate and House of Representatives, according to the rules and limitations prescribed in the case of a bill.

SECTION 8. The Congress shall have the power to lay and collect taxes, duties, imposts and excises, to pay the debts and provide for the common defence and general welfare of the United States; but all duties, imposts and excises shall be uniform throughout the United States:

To borrow money on the credit of the United States:

To regulate commerce with foreign nations, and among the several states, and with the Indian tribes:

To establish an uniform rule of naturalization, and uniform laws on the subject of bankruptcies throughout the United States:

To coin money, regulate the value thereof, and of foreign coin, and fix the standard of weights and measures:

To provide for the punishment of counterfeiting the securities and current coin of the United States:

To establish post-offices and post-roads:

To promote the progress of science and useful arts, by securing for limited times to authors and inventors the exclusive rights to their respective writings and discoveries:

To constitute tribunals inferior to the supreme court:

To define and punish piracies and felonies committed on the high seas, and offences against the law of nations:

To declare war, grant letters of marque and reprisal, and make rules concerning captures on land and water:

To raise and support armies, but no appropriation of money to that use shall be for a longer term than two years:

To provide and maintain a navy:

To make rules for the government and regulation of the land and naval forces:

To provide for calling forth the militia to execute the laws of the union, suppress insurrections and repel invasions:

To provide for organizing, arming and disciplining the militia, and for governing such part of them as may be employed in the service of the United States, reserving to the states respectively, the appointment of the officers, and the authority of training the militia according to the discipline prescribed by Congress:

To exercise exclusive legislation in all cases whatsoever, over such district (not exceeding ten miles square) as may, by cession of particular states, and the acceptance of Congress, become the seat of the government of the United States, and to exercise like authority over all places purchased by the consent of the legislature of the state in which the same shall be, for the erection of forts, magazines, arsenals, dock-yards, and other needful buildings:

And,

To make all laws which shall be necessary and proper for carrying into execution the foregoing powers, and all other powers vested by this constitution in the government of the United States, or in any department or officer thereof.

SECTION 9. The migration or importation of such persons as any of the states now existing shall think proper to admit, shall not be prohibited by the Congress prior to the year 1808, but a tax or duty may be imposed on such importation, not exceeding 10 dollars for each person.

The privilege of the writ of *habeas corpus* shall not be suspended, unless when in cases of rebellion or invasion the public safety may require it.

No bill of attainder or *ex post facto* law shall be passed.

No capitation, or other direct tax shall be laid unless in proportion to the census or enumeration herein before directed to be taken.

No tax or duty shall be laid on articles exported from any state.

No preference shall be given by any regulation of commerce or revenue to the ports of one state over those of another; nor shall vessels bound to, or from, one state, be obliged to enter, clear, or pay duties in another.

No money shall be drawn from the treasury, but in consequence of appropriations made by law; and a regular statement and account of the receipts and expenditures of all public money shall be published from time to time.

No title of nobility shall be granted by the United States: And no person holding any office of profit or trust under them, shall, without the consent of Congress, accept of any present, emolument, office, or title, of any kind whatever, from any king, prince or foreign state.

SECTION 10. No state shall enter into any treaty, alliance, or confederation; grant letters of marque and reprisal; coin money; emit bills of credit; make any thing but gold and silver coin a tender in payment of debts; pass any bill of attainder, *ex post facto* law, or law impairing the obligation of contracts, or grant any title of nobility.

No state shall, without the consent of Congress, lay any imposts or duties on imports or exports, except what may be absolutely necessary for executing its inspection laws; and the net produce of all duties and imposts, laid by any state on imports or exports, shall be for the use of the treasury of the United States; and all such laws shall be subject to the revision and control of the Congress.

No state shall, without the consent of Congress, lay any duty on tonnage, keep troops, or ships of war in time of peace, enter into any agreement or compact with another state, or with a foreign power, or engage in war, unless actually invaded, or in such imminent danger as will not admit of delay.

ARTICLE II.

SECTION 1. The executive power shall be vested in a president of the United States of America. He shall hold his office during the term of four years, and, together with the vice-president, chosen for the same term, be elected as follows:

Each state shall appoint, in such manner as the legislature thereof may direct, a number of electors, equal to the whole number of senators and representatives to which the state may be entitled in the Congress; but no senator or representative, or person holding an office of trust or profit under the United States, shall be appointed an elector.

The electors shall meet in their respective states, and vote by ballot for two persons, of whom one at least shall not be an inhabitant of the same state with themselves. And they shall make a list of all the persons voted for, and of the number of votes for each; which list they shall sign and certify, and transmit sealed to the seat of the government of the United States, directed to the president of the Senate. The president of the Senate shall, in the presence of the Senate and House of Representatives, open all the certificates and the votes shall then be counted. The person having the greatest number of votes shall be president, if such number be a majority of the whole number of electors appointed; and if there be more than one who have such majority, and have an equal number of votes, then the House of Representatives shall immediately choose by ballot one of them for president; and if no person have a majority, then from the five highest on the list, the said House shall, in like manner, choose the president. But in choosing the president, the votes shall be taken by states, the representation from each state having one vote; a quorum for this purpose shall consist of a member or members from two-thirds of the states, and a majority of all the states shall be necessary to a choice. In every case, after the choice of the president, the person having the greatest number of votes of the electors shall be the vice-president. But if there should remain two or more who have equal votes, the Senate shall choose from them by ballot the vice-president.

The Congress may determine the time of choosing the electors, and the day on which they shall give their votes; which day shall be the same throughout the United States.

No person except a natural born citizen, or a citizen of the United States, at the time of the adoption of this constitution, shall be eligible to the office of president; neither shall any person be eligible to that office, who shall not have attained to the age of 35 years, and been 14 years a resident within the United States.

In case of the removal of the president from office, or of his death, resignation, or inability to discharge the powers and duties of the said office, the same shall devolve on the vice-president, and the Congress may by law provide for the case of removal, death, resignation, or inability, both of the president and vice-president, declaring what officer shall then act as president, and such officer shall act accordingly, until the disability be removed, or a president shall be elected.

The president shall, at stated times, receive for his services, a compensation, which shall neither be increased nor diminished during the period for which he shall have been elected, and he shall not receive within that period any other emolument from the United States, or any of them.

Before he enter on the execution of his office, he shall take the following oath or affirmation:

"I do solemnly swear (or affirm) that I will faithfully execute the office of president of the United States, and will to the best of my ability, preserve, protect and defend the constitution of the United States."

SECTION 2. The president shall be commander in chief of the army and navy of the United States, and of the militia of the several states, when called into actual service of the United States; he may require the opinion, in writing, of the principal officer in each of the executive departments, upon any subject relating to the duties of their respective offices, and he shall have power to grant reprieves and pardons for offences against the United States, except in cases of impeachment.

He shall have power, by and with the advice and consent of the Senate, to make treaties, provided two-thirds of the senators present concur; and he shall nominate, and by and with the advice and consent of the Senate, shall appoint ambassadors, other public ministers and consuls, judges of the supreme court, and all other officers of the United States, whose appointments are not herein otherwise provided for, and which shall be established by law. But the Congress may by law vest the appointment of such inferior officers, as they think proper, in the president alone, in the courts of law, or in the heads of departments.

The president shall have power to fill up all vacancies that may happen during the recess of the Senate, by granting commissions, which shall expire at the end of their next session.

SECTION 3. He shall, from time to time, give to the Congress information of the state of the union, and recommend to their consideration, such measures as he shall judge necessary and expedient; he may, on extraordinary occasions, convene both houses, or either of them, and in case of disagreement between them, with respect to the time of adjournment, he may adjourn them to such time as he shall think proper; he shall receive ambassadors and other public ministers; he shall take care that the laws be faithfully executed, and shall commission all the officers of the United States.

SECTION 4. The president, vice-president, and all civil officers of the United States shall be removed from office on impeachment for, and conviction of, treason, bribery, or other high crimes and misdemeanors.

ARTICLE III.

SECTION 1. The judicial power of the United States, shall be vested in one supreme court, and in such inferior courts as the Congress may, from time to time, ordain and establish. The judges, both of the supreme and inferior courts, shall hold their offices during good behaviour, and shall, at stated times, receive for their services a compensation, which shall not be diminished during their continuance in office.

SECTION 2. The judicial power shall extend to all cases, in law and equity, arising under this constitution, the laws of the United States, and treaties made, or which shall be made under their authority; to all cases affecting ambassadors, other public ministers and consuls; to all cases of admiralty and maritime jurisdiction; to controversies to which the United States shall be a party: to controversies between two or more states, between a state and citizens of another state, between citizens of different states, between citizens of the same state, claiming lands under grants of different states, and between a state, or citizens thereof, and foreign states, citizens or subjects.

In all cases affecting ambassadors, other public ministers and consuls, and those in which a state shall be party, the supreme court shall have original jurisdiction. In all the other cases before-mentioned, the supreme court shall have appellate jurisdiction, both as to law and fact, with such exceptions, and under such regulations as the Congress shall make.

The trial of all crimes, except in cases of impeachment, shall be by jury; and such trial shall be held in the state where the said crimes shall have been committed; but when not committed within any state, the trial shall be at such place or places as the Congress may by law have directed.

SECTION 3. Treason against the United States shall consist only in levying war against them, or in adhering to their enemies, giving them aid and comfort. No person shall be convicted of treason unless on the testimony of two witnesses to the same overt act, or on confession in open court.

The Congress shall have power to declare the punishment of treason, but no attainder of treason shall work corruption of blood, or forfeiture, except during the life of the person attainted.

ARTICLE IV.

SECTION 1. Full faith and credit shall be given in each state to the public acts, records and judicial proceedings of every other state. And the Congress may by general laws prescribe the manner in which such acts, records and proceedings shall be proved, and the effect thereof.

SECTION 2. The citizens of each state shall be entitled to all privileges and immunities of citizens in the several states.

A person charged in any state with treason, felony, or other crime, who shall flee from justice, and be found in another state, shall, on demand of the executive authority of the state from which he fled, be delivered up, to be removed to the state having jurisdiction of the crime.

No person held to service or labour in one state, under the laws thereof, escaping into another, shall, in consequence of any law or regulation therein, be discharged from such service or labour, but shall be delivered up on claim of the party to whom such service or labour may be due.

SECTION 3. New states may be admitted by Congress into this union; but no new state shall be formed or erected within the jurisdiction of any other state, nor any state be formed by the junction of two or more states, or parts of states, without the consent of the legislatures of the states concerned, as well as of the Congress.

The Congress shall have power to dispose of and make all needful rules and regulations respecting the territory or other property belonging to the United States; and nothing in this constitution shall be so construed as to prejudice any claims of the United States, or of any particular state.

SECTION 4. The United States shall guarantee to every state in this union, a republican form of government, and shall protect each of them against invasion; and on application of the legislature, or of the executive (when the legislature cannot be convened), against domestic violence.

ARTICLE V.

The Congress, whenever two-thirds of both houses shall deem it necessary, shall propose amendments to this constitution, or on the application of the legislatures of two-thirds of the several states, shall call a convention for proposing amendments, which, in either case, shall be valid to all intents and purposes, as part of this constitution, when ratified by the legislatures of three-fourths of the several states, or by conventions in three-fourths thereof, as the one or the other mode of ratification may be proposed by the Congress: Provided, that no amendment which may be made prior to the year 1808, shall in any manner affect the first and fourth clauses in the ninth section of the first article; and that no state, without its consent, shall be deprived of its equal suffrage in the Senate.

ARTICLE VI.

All debts contracted and engagements entered into, before the adoption of this constitution, shall be as valid against the United States under this constitution, as under the confederation.

This constitution, and the laws of the United States which shall be made in pursuance thereof; and all treaties made, or which shall be made, under the authority of the United States shall be the supreme law of the land; and the judges in every state shall be bound thereby, any thing in the constitution or laws of any state to the contrary notwithstanding.

The senators and representatives before-mentioned, and the members of the several state legislatures, and all executive and judicial officers, both of the United States and of the several states, shall be bound by oath or affirmation, to support this constitution; but no religious test shall ever be required as a qualification to any office or public trust under the United States.

ARTICLE VII.

The ratification of the conventions of nine states, shall be sufficient for the establishment of this constitution between the states so ratifying the same.

Done in convention, by the unanimous consent of the states present, the 17th day of September, in the year of our Lord 1787, and of the independence of the United States of America the 12th. In witness whereof we have hereunto subscribed our names.

[Names omitted]

Articles of Amendment

AMENDMENT 1.

Congress shall make no law respecting an establishment of religion, or prohibiting the free exercise thereof; or abridging the freedom of speech or of the press; or the right of the people peaceably to assemble, and to petition the government for a redress of grievances.

AMENDMENT 2.

A well-regulated militia being necessary to the security of a free state, the right of the people to keep and bear arms shall not be infringed.

AMENDMENT 3.

No soldier shall, in time of peace, be quartered in any house without the consent of the owner, nor in time of war but in a manner to be prescribed by law.

AMENDMENT 4.

The right of the people to be secure in their persons, houses, papers, and effects, against unreasonable searches and seizures, shall not be violated, and no warrants shall issue but upon probable cause, supported by oath or affirmation, and particularly describing the place to be searched, and the persons or things to be seized.

AMENDMENT 5.

No person shall be held to answer for a capital or other infamous crime unless on a presentment or indictment of a grand jury, except in cases arising in the land or naval forces, or in the militia, when in actual service, in time of war or public danger; nor shall any person be subject for the same offence to be twice put in jeopardy of life or limb; nor shall be compelled in any criminal case to be a witness against himself, nor be deprived of life, liberty, or property, without due process of law; nor shall private property be taken for public use without just compensation.

AMENDMENT 6.

In all criminal prosecutions, the accused shall enjoy the right to a speedy and public trial, by an impartial jury of the state and district wherein the crime shall have been committed, which district shall have been previously ascertained by law, and to be informed of the nature and cause of the accusation; to be confronted with the witnesses against him; to have compulsory process for obtaining witnesses in his favor, and to have the assistance of counsel for his defense.

AMENDMENT 7.

In suits at common law, where the value in controversy shall exceed twenty dollars, the right of trial by jury shall be preserved, and no fact tried by a jury shall be otherwise re-examined in any court of the United States than according to the rules of the common law.

AMENDMENT 8.

Excessive bail shall not be required, nor excessive fines imposed, nor cruel and unusual punishments inflicted.

AMENDMENT 9.

The enumeration in the constitution of certain rights shall not be construed to deny or disparage others retained by the people.

AMENDMENT 10.

The powers not delegated to the United States by the constitution, nor prohibited by it to the states, are reserved to the states respectively, or to the people.

AMENDMENT 11.

The judicial power of the United States shall not be construed to extend to any suit in law or equity, commenced or prosecuted against one of the United States, by citizens of another state, or by citizens or subjects of any foreign state.

AMENDMENT 12.

The electors shall meet in their respective states, and vote by ballot for President and Vice-President, one of whom at least shall not be an inhabitant of the same state with themselves; they shall name in their ballots the person voted for as President, and in distinct ballots the person voted for as Vice-President; and they shall make distinct lists of all persons voted for as President, and of all persons voted for as Vice-President, and of the number of votes for each, which lists they shall sign and certify, and transmit, sealed, to the seat of the government of the United States directed to the president of the Senate; the president of the Senate shall, in the presence of the Senate and House of Representatives, open all the certificates, and the votes shall then be counted; the person having the greatest number of votes for President shall be the President, if such number be a majority of the whole number of electors appointed; and if no person have such majority, then from the persons having the highest numbers not exceeding three, on the list of those voted for as President, the House of Representatives shall choose immediately, by ballot, the President. But in choosing the President, the votes shall be taken by states, the representation from each state having one vote; a quorum for this purpose shall consist of a member or members from two-thirds of the states, and a majority of all the states shall be necessary to a choice. And if the House of Representatives shall not choose a President, whenever the right of choice shall devolve upon them, before the fourth day of March next following, then the Vice-President shall act as President, as in the case of the death or other constitutional disability of the President. The person having the greatest number of votes as Vice-President shall be the Vice-President, if such number be a majority of the whole number of electors appointed, and if no person have a majority, then from the two highest numbers on the list the Senate shall choose the Vice-President; a quorum for the purpose shall consist of two-thirds of the whole number of senators, and a majority of the whole number shall be necessary to a choice. But no person constitutionally ineligible to the office of President shall be eligible to that of Vice-President of the United States.

AMENDMENT 13.

SECTION 1. Neither slavery nor involuntary servitude, except as a punishment for crime whereof the party shall have been duly convicted, shall exist within the United States, or any place subject to their jurisdiction.

SECTION 2. Congress shall have power to enforce this article by appropriate legislation.

AMENDMENT 14.

SECTION 1. All persons born or naturalized in the United States, and subject to the jurisdiction thereof, are citizens of the United States and of the state wherein they reside. No state shall make or enforce any law which shall abridge the privileges or immunities of citizens of the United States; nor shall any state deprive any person of life, liberty, or property without due process of law; nor deny to any person within its jurisdiction the equal protection of the law.

SECTION 2. Representatives shall be apportioned among the several States according to their respective numbers, counting the whole number of persons in each state, excluding Indians not taxed. But when the right to vote at any election for the choice of electors for President and Vice-President of the United States, representatives in Congress, the executive and judicial officers of a State, or the members of the legislature thereof, is denied to any of the male members of such state being of twenty-one years of age, and citizens of the United States, or in any way abridged, except for participation in rebellion or other crime, the basis of representation therein shall be reduced in the proportion which the number of such male citizens shall bear to the whole number of male citizens twenty-one years of age in such state.

SECTION 3. No person shall be a senator or representative in Congress, or elector of President and Vice-President, or hold any office, civil or military, under the United States, or under any state, who, having previously taken an oath, as a member of Congress, or as an officer of the United States, or as a member of any state legislature, or as an executive or judicial officer of any state, to support the Constitution of the United States, shall have engaged in insurrection or rebellion against the same, or given aid and comfort to the enemies thereof. But Congress may, by a vote of two-thirds of each House, remove such disability.

SECTION 4. The validity of the public debt of the United States, authorized by law, including debts incurred for payment of pensions and bounties for services in suppressing insurrection or rebellion, shall not be questioned. But neither the United States nor any state shall assume or pay any debt or obligation incurred in aid of insurrection or rebellion against the United States, or any claim for the loss or emancipation of any slave; but all such debts, obligations, and claims shall be held illegal and void.

SECTION 5. The Congress shall have power to enforce, by appropriate legislation, the provisions of this article.

AMENDMENT 15.

SECTION 1. The right of citizens of the United States to vote shall not be denied or abridged by the United States or by any state, on account of race, color, or previous condition of servitude.

SECTION 2. The Congress shall have power to enforce this article by appropriate legislation.

AMENDMENT 16.

The Congress shall have power to lay and collect taxes on incomes, from whatever source derived, without apportionment among the several States, and without regard to any census or enumeration.

AMENDMENT 17.

The Senate of the United States shall be composed of two senators from each state, elected by the people thereof for six years; and each senator shall have one vote. The electors in each state shall have the qualifications requisite for electors of the most numerous branch of the state legislatures.

When vacancies happen in the representation of any state in the Senate, the executive authority of such state shall issue writs of election to fill such vacancies; provided, that the legislature of any state may empower the executive thereof to make temporary appointments until the people fill the vacancies by election as the legislature may direct.

This amendment shall not be so construed as to affect the election or term of any senator chosen before it becomes valid as part of the Constitution.

AMENDMENT 18.

SECTION 1. After one year from the ratification of this article the manufacture, sale, or transportation of intoxicating liquors within, the importation thereof into, or exportation thereof from the United States and all territory subject to the jurisdiction thereof, for beverage purposes is hereby prohibited.

SECTION 2. The Congress and the several states shall have concurrent power to enforce this article by appropriate legislation.

SECTION 3. This article shall be inoperative unless it shall have been ratified as an amendment to the Constitution by the legislatures of the several states, as provided in the Constitution, within seven years from the date of submission hereof to the states by the Congress.

AMENDMENT 19.

The right of the citizens of the United States to vote shall not be denied or abridged by the United States or by any state on account of sex.

Congress shall have power to enforce this article by appropriate legislation.

AMENDMENT 20.

SECTION 1. The terms of the President and Vice-President shall end at noon on the 20th day of January, and the terms of senators and representatives at noon on the 3rd day of January, of the year in which such terms would have ended if this article had not been ratified; and the terms of their successors shall then begin.

SECTION 2. The Congress shall assemble at least once in every year, and such meeting shall begin at noon on the 3rd day of January, unless they shall by law appoint a different day.

SECTION 3. If, at the time fixed for the beginning of the term of President, the President elect shall have died, the Vice-President elect shall become President. If a President shall not have been chosen before the time fixed for the beginning of his term, or if the President elect shall have failed to qualify, then the Vice-President elect shall act as President until a President shall have qualified; and the Congress may by law provide for the case wherein neither a President elect nor a Vice-President elect shall have qualified, declaring who shall then act as President, or the manner in which one who is to act shall be selected, and such person shall act accordingly until a President or Vice-President shall have qualified.

SECTION 4. The Congress may by law provide for the case of the death of any of the persons from whom the House of Representatives may choose a President, whenever the right of choice shall have devolved upon them, and for the case of the death of any of the persons from whom the Senate may choose a Vice-President, whenever the right of choice shall have devolved upon them.

SECTION 5. Sections 1 and 2 shall take effect on the 15th day of October following the ratification of this article.

SECTION 6. This article shall be inoperative unless it shall have been ratified as an amendment to the Constitution by the legislatures of three-fourths of the several states within seven years from the date of its submission.

AMENDMENT 21.

SECTION 1. The eighteenth article of amendment to the Constitution of the United States is hereby repealed.

SECTION 2. The transportation or importation into any state, territory, or possession of the United States, for delivery or use therein of intoxicating liquors, in violation of the laws thereof, is hereby prohibited.

SECTION 3. This article shall be inoperative unless it shall have been ratified as an amendment to the Constitution by conventions in the several states, as provided in the Constitution, within seven years from the date of the submission hereof to the states by the Congress.

AMENDMENT 22.

No person shall be elected to the office of the President more than twice, and no person who has held the office of President, or acted as President, for more than two years of a term to which some other person was elected President shall be elected to the office of the President more than once. But this Article shall not apply to any person holding the office of President when this Article was proposed by the Congress, and shall not prevent any person who may be holding the office of President, or acting as President, during the term within which this Article becomes operative from holding the office of President or acting as President during the remainder of such term.

AMENDMENT 23.

SECTION 1. The District constituting the seat of Government of the United States shall appoint in such manner as the Congress may direct:

A number of electors of President and Vice-President equal to the whole number of Senators and Representatives in Congress to which the District would be entitled if it were a State, but in no event more than the least populous State; they shall be in addition to those appointed by the States, but they shall be considered, for the purpose of the election of President and Vice-President, to be electors appointed by a State; and they shall meet in the District and perform such duties as provided by the twelfth article of amendment.

SECTION 2. The Congress shall have power to enforce this article by appropriate legislation.

AMENDMENT 24.

SECTION 1. The right of citizens of the United States to vote in any primary or other election for President or Vice-President, for electors for President or Vice-President, or for Senator or Representative in Congress, shall not be denied or abridged by the United States or any State by reason of failure to pay any poll tax or other tax.

SECTION 2. The Congress shall have power to enforce this article by appropriate legislation.

AMENDMENT 25.

SECTION 1. In case of the removal of the President from office or of his death or resignation, the Vice-President shall become President.

SECTION 2. Whenever there is a vacancy in the office of the Vice-President, the President shall nominate a Vice-President who shall take office upon confirmation by a majority vote of both Houses of Congress.

SECTION 3. Whenever the President transmits to the President pro tempore of the Senate and the Speaker of the House of Representatives his written declaration that he is unable to discharge the powers and duties of his office, and until he transmits to them a written declaration to the contrary, such powers and duties shall be discharged by the Vice-President as Acting President.

SECTION 4.   Whenever the Vice-President and a majority of either the principal officers of the executive departments or of such other body as Congress may by law provide, transmit to the President pro tempore of the Senate and the Speaker of the House of Representatives their written declaration that the President is unable to discharge the powers and duties of his office, the Vice-President shall immediately assume the powers and duties of the office as Acting President.

Thereafter, when the President transmits to the President pro tempore of the Senate and the Speaker of the House of Representatives his written declaration that no inability exists, he shall resume the powers and duties of his office unless the Vice-President and a majority of either the principal officers of the executive departments or of such other body as Congress may by law provide, transmit within four days to the President pro tempore of the Senate and the Speaker of the House of Representatives their written declaration that the President is unable to discharge the powers and duties of his office. Thereupon Congress shall decide the issue, assembling within forty-eight hours for that purpose if not in session. If the Congress, within twenty-one days after receipt of the latter written declaration, or, if Congress is not in session, within twenty-one days after Congress is required to assemble, determines by two-thirds vote of both Houses that the President is unable to discharge the powers and duties of his office, the Vice-President shall continue to discharge the same as Acting President; otherwise, the President shall resume the powers and duties of his office.

AMENDMENT 26.

SECTION 1.   The right of citizens of the United States, who are eighteen years or older, to vote shall not be denied or abridged by the United States or any State on account of age.

SECTION 2.   The Congress shall have the power to enforce this article by appropriate legislation.

PART VI:

Know Your Q's and A's

Study these questions and answers.

1. Q. What is the United States Constitution?
   A. The supreme (highest) law of the United States.
2. Q. When was it written?
   A. May to September 1787.
3. Q. Who wrote it?
   A. Gouverneur Morris wrote it in its final form, but it was the outgrowth of ideas and compromises of the delegates who attended the Constitutional Convention in Philadelphia. Among the leaders were George Washington, James Madison, Benjamin Franklin, and Alexander Hamilton.
4. Q. How many delegates attended the Constitutional Convention?
   A. Fifty-five, from twelve of the thirteen states that were then the United States.
5. Q. What state did not send a delegate?
   A. Rhode Island.
6. Q. How many of the delegates signed the Constitution?
   A. Thirty-nine.
7. Q. When was the Constitution adopted?
   A. July 2, 1788, but it did not go into effect until March 4, 1789.

8. Q. How many states had to ratify before it was adopted?
   A. Nine of the thirteen: three fourths of the states.
9. Q. By what date had nine states ratified it?
   A. June 21, 1788.
10. Q. What is the Preamble to the Constitution?
    A. An introduction listing six reasons for writing the Constitution.
11. Q. What are the six reasons listed in the Preamble?
    A. To form a more perfect union, establish justice, insure domestic tranquillity, provide for the common defense, promote the general welfare, and secure the blessings of liberty for ourselves and our posterity.
12. Q. What are the three branches of our federal government?
    A. The legislative branch, the executive branch, and the judicial branch.
13. Q. Where in the Constitution do we find information about the legislative branch?
    A. Article I; Amendments 16, 17, and 20.
14. Q. What is the legislative branch?
    A. Congress.
15. Q. What is Congress?
    A. The lawmaking body of our national government.
16. Q. Of what is Congress composed?
    A. Two houses, the House of Representatives and the Senate.
17. Q. How is membership in the House of Representatives determined?
    A. By the populations of the various states.
18. Q. How many representatives are there?
    A. 435 ordinarily.
19. Q. Approximately how many people does each representative represent?
    A. About 521,000.
20. Q. Why does each representative represent so many people?
    A. Congress passed a law limiting the number of

representatives to 435 in 1929, to keep the House from growing so large it could not operate effectively.

21. Q. How do representatives get their offices?
    A. They are elected by the people of their states.

22. Q. What qualifications must a person meet to be a representative?
    A. He must be at least twenty-five years of age, have been a citizen of the United States for at least seven years, and must live in the district of the state he represents.

23. Q. What requirements must a person meet to be a voter in most states?
    A. He must be a citizen of the United States and of the state in which he lives, must have reached eighteen years of age, and must be registered to vote.

24. Q. How do we know the population of each state?
    A. The federal government takes a census every ten years (on the "zero" years).

25. Q. How long is a representative's term of office?
    A. Two years.

26. Q. What happens if a representative dies in office, or for some other reason must vacate his office?
    A. The governor of his state calls a special election to replace him.

27. Q. Who is chairman of the House?
    A. The Speaker of the House.

28. Q. Who are some of the other officers of the House?
    A. The chaplain, the sergeant at arms, the clerk, and the parliamentarian.

29. Q. How are these officers chosen?
    A. They are nominated by a caucus of the majority party in the House and elected by the members of the House.

30. Q. How is representation in the Senate determined?
    A. By equal representation, two senators from each state.

31. Q. How many senators are there?
    A. One hundred.
32. Q. How do senators get their offices?
    A. They are elected by the people of their states, the same as representatives.
33. Q. What qualifications must a person meet to be a senator?
    A. He must be at least thirty years of age, have been a citizen of the United States for at least nine years, and live in the state he represents.
34. Q. Have senators always been elected by the people?
    A. No, originally only the House was elected by the people. The senators were chosen in each state by the state legislatures. Amendment 17, ratified in 1913, gave the people of the states the right to elect senators.
35. Q. How long is a senator's term of office?
    A. Six years, but we elect one third of the senators every two years on the same day we elect representatives.
36. Q. How is this possible?
    A. The first Senate was divided into three groups. One group was to serve two years, one four years, and one six years.
37. Q. Why was this done?
    A. To always have experienced men in the Senate.
38. Q. What happens if a senator dies in office, or for some reason must vacate his office?
    A. The governor of his state, with the permission of the state legislature, may appoint a temporary senator, or he may call a special election to replace him.
39. Q. Who is chairman of the Senate?
    A. The Vice-President of the United States.
40. Q. How can the Vice-President be the chairman of the Senate?
    A. The Constitution makes this a duty of the Vice-President. Remember, the Senate was not elected by the people at first.

41. Q. Can the Vice-President vote in the Senate?
    A. No, except to break a tie vote.
42. Q. What is the Vice-President called when he presides over the Senate?
    A. President of the Senate.
43. Q. Who acts as chairman of the Senate if the Vice-President, for some reason, cannot be present?
    A. The president pro tempore of the Senate.
44. Q. Who are some of the other officers of the Senate?
    A. The chaplain, the sergeant at arms, the secretary, and the clerk.
45. Q. How are officers elected?
    A. By the senators.
46. Q. What is an impeachment trial?
    A. A trial to remove a public official from office.
47. Q. Who does the impeaching?
    A. The House of Representatives has the sole power of impeachment (accusing the official).
48. Q. Who tries an impeachment case?
    A. The Senate has the sole power of trying impeachment cases.
49. Q. What is a quorum in the Senate for the purpose of trying impeachments?
    A. Two thirds of the senators.
50. Q. How large a vote does it take to convict an official being tried for impeachment?
    A. Two thirds of all the senators present.
51. Q. Who may be impeached?
    A. Any public official except a member of either house of Congress.
52. Q. How is a congressman removed from office?
    A. He is expelled by a two-thirds vote of his house.
53. Q. How may an impeached official be punished if he is found guilty?
    A. There is no punishment except removal from office and the right to ever hold another office of the United States.
54. Q. What if he has committed a crime?

A. After the impeachment trial he may be tried in the regular courts.

55. Q. Is it fair for the Vice-President to preside over the Senate at the impeachment trial of a President, when he is next in line for that office?
A. The Vice-President does not preside over the impeachment trial of a President; the Chief Justice of the United States does.

56. Q. When are congressmen elected?
A. The Tuesday after the first Monday in November of even-numbered years.

57. Q. When do congressmen take office?
A. January 3 following the election in November.

58. Q. Who judges the qualifications of persons elected to Congress?
A. Each house judges its newly elected members and may refuse by a majority vote to let an unqualified person take his seat.

59. Q. What is a quorum for business in each house?
A. A majority of the members.

60. Q. How do we know what happens in Congress?
A. Each house keeps a journal of what it does each day, and the information from these journals is published in the *Congressional Record* each day Congress is in session.

61. Q. Is everything said and done published in the *Congressional Record?*
A. No, some matters may be kept secret, if necessary.

62. Q. Do both houses always meet at the same time?
A. Yes, the Constitution requires them to meet at the same time and place; and neither house may adjourn for more than three days without the consent of the other.

63. Q. How often must Congress meet?
A. At least once a year, but they usually hold meetings for about nine months out of the year.

64. Q. Are congressmen paid for their services?
A. Yes, they receive $60,662.50 a year. The Speaker of the House receives $79,125 a year.

65. Q. What is congressional immunity?

A. No congressman may be arrested in or going to or from either house of Congress except for treason, felony, or breach of peace; and no congressman may be sued for what he says on the floor of either house.

66. Q. May congressmen hold other offices in the United States government?

A. No congressman may accept any United States office that has been set up or any that has had an increase in salary during the time he is in office. No person, while still holding any United States office, may be a congressman.

67. Q. What is a bill?

A. A proposed law.

68. Q. How does a bill become a law?

A. It must pass both houses of Congress by a majority vote and be signed by the President.

69. Q. What is a veto?

A. The President's power to refuse to sign a bill, and to send it back to the house where it originated, along with his objections to it.

70. Q. What happens if the President vetoes a bill?

A. It is returned to the house where it originated. It must then receive a two-thirds vote in each house to become a law without the President's signature. If this is done, we call it overriding the veto. If not, we call it sustaining the veto.

71. Q. What if the President neither signs nor vetoes a bill?

A. It becomes a law without his signature in ten days (Sundays not counted) unless Congress adjourns within that time. In that case, it does not become a law. We say it has received a "pocket veto."

72. Q. Can a bill originate in either house of Congress?

A. Yes, except for a tax bill, which must originate in the House of Representatives.

73. Q. May either house amend a bill of the other?

A. Yes, but it must be returned to the house where it originated, and that house may agree to the

amendments or make further amendments of
its own.

74. Q. Must the President see resolutions passed by
Congress, as well as bills?

A. Yes, except for (1) a resolution to adjourn,
(2) a nonlegislative resolution, or (3) a joint
resolution for proposing an amendment to the
Constitution.

75. Q. Why must the President see resolutions made
by Congress?

A. To keep from being bypassed by a law that
Congress has called a resolution.

76. Q. How are resolutions passed?

A. In the same manner as bills.

77. Q. What are some of the expressed powers of Congress?

A. To tax, to borrow money, to regulate commerce, to make naturalization and bankruptcy
laws, to coin money, to fix the standard of
weights and measures, to punish counterfeiters,
to establish post offices and post roads, to make
copyright and patent laws, to establish federal
courts, to punish crimes at sea, to declare war,
to raise and support armed forces (army, navy,
air force), to organize and regulate states'
militias, and to control the District of Columbia
and all United States government property in
the states.

78. Q. What is meant by the "implied" powers of
Congress?

A. The power given by the "elastic clause," which
says that Congress may pass any law needed to
see that its powers are carried out.

79. Q. What powers are forbidden to Congress?

A. To take away writs of *habeas corpus*, to pass
ex post facto laws or bills of attainder, to tax
exports, to give advantages to ports of any
state, to tax goods shipped by water to or from
a state, to withdraw money from the Treasury
without an act of Congress, to fail to account

for and make public all money received and
spent, or to grant titles of nobility.

80. Q. What powers are forbidden to the states?
    A. To make treaties, alliances, or confederations,
       to grant letters of marque and reprisal, to coin
       or print money, to back money with anything
       other than gold and silver, to pass bills of at-
       tainder, *ex post facto* laws, or laws destroying
       the obligation of contracts; and without Con-
       gress' consent, grant titles of nobility, tax im-
       ports or exports, except to pay inspection fees,
       tax tonnage, keep troops or warships in peace-
       time, make treaties or compacts with other
       states or foreign countries, or fight a war ex-
       cept when attacked.

81. Q. Where can information about the executive
       branch be found in the Constitution?
    A. Article II; Amendments 12, 20, 22, 23, and 25.

82. Q. What is the executive branch?
    A. The President, the Vice-President, and the
       President's Cabinet, and all other departments
       under the President.

83. Q. What is the President's main function?
    A. To see that United States laws are enforced, or
       carried out.

84. Q. Who elects the President and Vice-President?
    A. The electoral college.

85. Q. What is the electoral college?
    A. All the electors in the United States.

86. Q. What is an elector?
    A. A person elected by the people of a state to
       cast a vote for President and Vice-President.

87. Q. How do electors vote?
    A. They meet in their state capitals, cast a vote
       for a presidential and a vice-presidential candi-
       date by name, make a list of the number of
       votes cast for each candidate for each office,
       sign, seal, and certify the ballots, and send
       them to the President of the Senate in Wash-
       ington, D. C.

88. Q. How are the electoral votes from all the states counted?
    A. They are counted in the presence of both houses of Congress.
89. Q. How many electors are there?
    A. One for each senator and each representative from each state, plus three in the District of Columbia—a total of 538.
90. Q. How are a President and Vice-President elected?
    A. The presidential and vice-presidential candidates who receive a majority of the electoral votes cast for each office are elected.
91. Q. What if no presidential candidate has a majority?
    A. The House of Representatives elects a President from the three candidates with the most electoral votes for that office. A quorum in the House for this purpose is one or more members from two thirds of the states. The vote is taken by state ballot and each state has one vote. A majority of the states is necessary to elect a President.
92. Q. What if no vice-presidential candidate gets a majority of electoral votes?
    A. The Senate elects a Vice-President from the two candidates with the most electoral votes for that office. A quorum in the Senate for this purpose is two thirds of the senators. Each senator has one vote, and a majority vote is necessary to elect a Vice-President.
93. Q. When are electors elected?
    A. The Tuesday after the first Monday in November of every fourth year.
94. Q. When do electors vote?
    A. The Monday after the second Wednesday in December following the election.
95. Q. When does Congress count the electoral votes?
    A. January 6 following the election unless that day is Sunday, in which case, it is the next day.

96. Q. How long are the terms of office for President and Vice-President?
    A. Four years each.
97. Q. How many terms may a President serve?
    A. Two unless he has served or acted as President for more than half a term to which someone else was elected. In that case, he may serve only one more term. He may serve two more full terms if he has served or acted as President for less than half a term to which someone else was elected.
98. Q. What qualifications must a person meet to be elected President?
    A. He must be a natural-born citizen, be at least thirty-five years of age, and have lived in the United States at least fourteen years.
99. Q. What is meant by presidential succession?
    A. The order in which persons are to fill the office during a term if the President dies, resigns, or is removed from office.
100. Q. What is the line of succession?
    A. Vice-President; Speaker of the House; president pro tempore of the Senate; the President's Cabinet in the order of the establishment of their offices except for the Secretary of Health and Human Services, the Secretary of Housing and Urban Development, and the Secretary of Transportation, who are not included.
101. Q. Is the President paid for his services?
    A. Yes, he receives $200,000 a year, plus $165,000 in expense allowances.
102. Q. Is the Vice-President paid for his services?
    A. Yes, he receives $79,125 a year, plus $10,000 in expense allowances.
103. Q. What is the inauguration of the President?
    A. The ceremony in which the President-elect accepts the office by taking the presidential oath.
104. Q. What is the President's oath of office?
    A. "I do solemnly swear (or affirm) that I will faithfully execute the office of President of the

United States, and will to the best of my ability, preserve, protect and defend the constitution of the United States."

105. Q. What happens if a President-elect dies before he takes office?

A. The Vice-President-elect becomes President.

106. Q. What happens if the President-elect cannot qualify for the office, or if no President has been elected by the time that the President must take office?

A. The Vice-President acts as President until the time a President qualifies or is elected.

107. Q. What happens if neither the President-elect nor the Vice-President-elect can qualify for office?

A. Congress may direct, by law, who shall act as President, or the manner in which an acting President may be chosen. The Acting President shall serve until a qualified President or Vice-President is elected.

108. Q. What happens when the House must elect a President, and one or more of the presidential candidates from among the three with the most electoral votes dies; and what happens when the Senate must elect a Vice-President, and either or both of the candidates with the highest number of electoral votes dies?

A. Congress may provide for these cases by law. It has not yet done so.

109. Q. What are some of the powers and duties of the President?

A. To be Commander in Chief of the armed forces; to require written reports from the heads of the executive departments; to grant reprieves and pardons except for impeachment cases; to make treaties, with the consent of two thirds of the Senate; to appoint ambassadors, public ministers, consuls, Supreme Court judges, and other officers of the United States, with the consent of the Senate; to make temporary appointments, without the Senate's consent, if the Senate has recessed; to make a "state of the union" message to Congress each session; to convene either or both houses of Congress on extraordinary occasions; to adjourn Congress, if the houses of Congress cannot agree on a date for adjournment; to receive ambassadors and other public ministers; to see that our laws are faithfully executed; and to commission all officers of the United States.

110. Q. How may a President or Vice-President be removed from office?
A. By impeachment, and conviction of treason bribery, other high crimes, or misdemeanors.

111. Q. What is the President's Cabinet?
A. Persons who head certain executive departments and act as advisers to the President.

112. Q. How are Cabinet members chosen?
A. They are appointed by the President, with the consent of the Senate.

113. Q. How long do they serve?
A. No set period of time.

114. Q. Are they paid for their services?
A. Yes, $69,630 a year.

115. Q. What are the Cabinet officers?
A. (1) Secretary of State, (2) Secretary of the Treasury, (3) Secretary of Defense, (4) Attorney General, (5) Secretary of the Interior, (6) Secretary of Agriculture, (7) Secretary of Commerce, (8) Secretary of Labor, (9) Secretary of Health and Human Services, (10) Secretary of Housing and Urban Development, (11) Secretary of Transportation, (12) Secretary of Energy, and (13) Secretary of Education.

116. Q. Where can information concerning the judicial branch be found in the Constitution.
A. Article III; Amendment 11.

117. Q. What is the judicial branch?
A. The Supreme Court of the United States and all other federal courts.

118. Q. How are federal courts set up?
A. The Constitution establishes the Supreme

Court, and Congress establishes all those under the Supreme Court (inferior federal courts).

119. Q. What is the main function of the federal courts?
   A. To interpret the laws of the United States.

120. Q. What kinds of federal courts are there?
   A. Regular federal courts and special federal courts.

121. Q. What are regular federal courts?
   A. Federal courts that hear and try criminal, civil, and equity cases.

122. Q. What are special federal courts?
   A. Federal courts that hear and judge civil and equity cases of certain specific types.

123. Q. How many regular and special federal courts are there?
   A. Three of each.

124. Q. What are the three regular federal courts?
   A. The Supreme Court, the court of appeals, and the district courts.

125. Q. What are the four special federal courts?
   A. Court of Claims, Court of Customs and Patent Appeals, Court of International Trade, and the Tax Court.

126. Q. How long do federal judges serve?
   A. For life or during good behavior.

127. Q. What is meant by the jurisdiction of a court?
   A. The power of a court to hear and try certain kinds of cases.

128. Q. Over what kinds of cases do the federal courts have jurisdiction?
   A. All cases concerning the Constitution and the laws and treaties of the United States; all cases affecting ambassadors, public ministers, and consuls; all cases concerning crimes at sea; all cases concerning controversies to which the United States is a party; and all cases concerning controversies between two or more states, between citizens of different states, and between citizens of the same state claiming lands under grants of different states.

129. Q. What is meant by original jurisdiction?

A. The power of a court to try certain cases first.

130. Q. What is meant by appellate jurisdiction?
A. The power of a court to retry a case already tried in a lower court.

131. Q. Does the Supreme Court have both original and appellate jurisdiction?
A. Yes.

132. Q. Over what kinds of cases does the Supreme Court have original jurisdiction?
A. Cases affecting ambassadors, public ministers, and consuls; and cases concerning disputes between states.

133. Q. Over what kind of cases does the Supreme Court have appellate jurisdiction?
A. All the other cases mentioned in the Constitution.

134. Q. What are the judges of the Supreme Court called?
A. Justices.

135. Q. How many are there?
A. Nine, one Chief Justice and eight associate justices.

136. Q. Are Supreme Court justices paid for their services?
A. Yes, the Chief Justice receives $96,800 a year, and the associate justices receive $93,000 a year. Their salaries cannot be lowered while they hold office.

137. Q. What are the salaries of other federal judges?
A. Judges of the courts of appeals, Court of Claims, and Court of Customs and Patent Appeals receive $74,300 a year. Judges of the district courts, the Court of International Trade, and the Tax Court receive $70,300 a year. Their salaries cannot be lowered while they hold office.

138. Q. What is treason?
A. Making war against the United States or helping the enemies of the United States.

139. Q. What is necessary to convict a person of treason?

A. The testimony of two persons who saw the accused person commit an open act of treason, or a confession to the act by the accused.

140. Q. How is a traitor punished?
A. Usually by death or imprisonment, but a convicted traitor's family cannot be made to suffer for his crime, nor can his property be confiscated, except during his lifetime.

141. Q. Do states recognize the laws, records, and court decisions of other states?
A. Yes, but only in matters concerning civil law. No state tries to enforce the criminal laws of another state unless they happen to be the same in that state.

142. Q. Do citizens of one state have the same rights and protections in all the other states?
A. Yes, but they are not allowed to vote in another state unless they first become a citizen of that state.

143. Q. What is meant by extradition?
A. The return of a fugitive from justice from one state, by the governor of that state, to the state from which he escaped, at the request of the governor of that state.

144. Q. Who admits new states to the Union?
A. Congress, but no new state may be made by dividing a state, or by combining or taking parts of two or more states, without the consent of Congress and the states' legislatures involved.

145. Q. Who controls and makes rules for all United States territories and other government-owned property?
A. Congress.

146. Q. What three guarantees are made to the states by Congress?
A. A republican (representative) form of government, protection against invasion, and when asked for, protection against riots and mob action.

147. Q. How may an amendment to the Constitution be proposed?
  A. By a two-thirds vote of both houses of Congress or by a convention called by Congress at the request of two thirds of the states' legislatures.

148. Q. How may a proposed amendment be ratified?
  A. By three fourths of the states' legislatures or by special constitutional conventions held in three fourths of the states.

149. Q. What amendment cannot be proposed?
  A. An amendment to take away any state's right to equal representation in the Senate, without that state's consent.

150. Q. If a state constitution or state law conflicts with the United States Constitution or a United States law or treaty, which does away with the other?
  A. The United States Constitution and United States laws and treaties must be obeyed over any state constitution or state law.

151. Q. How do the laws of the United States rank in this respect?
  A. (1) The United States Constitution, (2) United States laws and treaties, (3) state constitutions, (4) state laws, (5) local laws.

152. Q. Which is higher, United States laws or treaties?
  A. Neither; whichever is more recent applies.

153. Q. What are all officers of the United States government and of the states' governments required to do?
  A. Take an oath to support the United States Constitution.

154. Q. What is the Bill of Rights?
  A. The first ten amendments to the Constitution.

155. Q. When was it ratified?
  A. December 15, 1791.

156. Q. Why was it written?
  A. The people of the United States wanted their personal rights written into the Constitution.

157. Q. What five freedoms are guaranteed to the people by Amendment 1?
   A. Freedom of religion, speech, press, assembly, and petition.

158. Q. Why are people given the right to bear arms?
   A. So the states may have well-trained militias.

159. Q. May Congress order soldiers to be quartered in private homes?
   A. Not in peacetime, and only by law in wartime.

160. Q. What is a warrant?
   A. A court order allowing a person to be arrested or searched; or allowing his property to be searched or seized; or all of these things.

161. Q. May people and their property be searched and seized?
   A. Only if a warrant has been sworn against them stating who and what may be searched or seized, and where the search or seizure is to take place.

162. Q. What protections does a person accused of a crime have?
   A. He must be indicted by a grand jury, he cannot be placed in double jeopardy, he cannot be made to give evidence against himself, and he may not be executed, imprisoned, or fined except by due process of law.

163. Q. What is meant by double jeopardy?
   A. If a person has been tried and found innocent, he cannot be tried again for the same crime.

164. Q. What is meant by due process of law?
   A. Fair court actions based upon fair laws.

165. Q. May the United States government take private property for public use?
   A. Yes, but a fair price must be paid for it.

166. Q. What rights does a person accused of a crime have?
   A. The right to a public trial as soon as possible, to an impartial jury, to hear charges made against him, to hear witnesses against him, to call witnesses to testify for him, and to a lawyer's services.

167. Q. May a person involved in a civil suit have a jury trial?

A. Yes, if the value of the object of dispute is more than twenty dollars.

168. Q. May a person be required to pay unreasonably high bail or fines?

A. No.

169. Q. What types of punishment may not be used against persons convicted of a crime?

A. Cruel or unusual punishments, such as torture or branding.

170. Q. Are all the rights of the people listed in the Constitution?

A. No, they are too numerous to list.

171. Q. What is meant by the "reserved" powers of the states?

A. Any powers not exclusive powers of Congress nor specifically denied to the states are powers reserved for the states.

172. Q. What two types of cases that were once under the jurisdiction of the federal courts are denied to the federal courts by Amendment 11?

A. The right to try cases involving a dispute between a state and citizens of that state; and disputes between a state and a foreign country, or citizens or subjects of a foreign country.

173. Q. Where are these cases tried?

A. In the state courts.

174. Q. Amendment 13 ended what terrible wrong?

A. Slavery.

175. Q. Are all persons born or naturalized in the United States citizens of the United States and the state in which they live?

A. Yes, of the United States, and of the state, provided they have lived in the state long enough.

176. Q. May a state take away life, liberty, or property without due process of law?

A. No.

177. Q. May a person be denied the right to vote because of his color or race?

A. No.

178. Q. What direct tax is provided for by Amendment 16?
A. The federal income tax.

179. Q. What is the income tax?
A. A tax on earnings—the more earned, the greater the percentage of the earnings collected by the tax.

180. Q. What was national "prohibition"?
A. Amendment 18 made illegal the manufacture, sale, or transportation of intoxicating liquors.

181. Q. How long did this last?
A. 1919–1933.

182. Q. What ended national "prohibition"?
A. Amendment 21 repealed Amendment 18. This ended "prohibition."

183. Q. May states have "prohibition"?
A. Yes.

184. Q. Do any states have "prohibition"?
A. No. Some counties within states have it.

185. Q. Have women always had the right to vote in the United States?
A. No, they were given this right by Amendment 19 in 1920.

186. Q. Have the people of the District of Columbia always voted in presidential elections?
A. No.

187. Q. Why not?
A. It is not a state and has no representatives or senators, so it was not entitled to any electors until the Constitution was amended in 1961.

188. Q. What is a poll tax?
A. A voting tax collected to pay the cost of holding an election, and in some cases, to prevent certain citizens, who cannot afford to pay, from voting.

189. Q. May a state have a poll tax?
A. No, not in federal elections.

190. Q. What happens when a vacancy occurs in the office of Vice-President?

A. The President nominates a Vice-President who must be confirmed by a majority vote of both houses of Congress.

191. Q. What if the President is unable to carry out the powers and duties of his office?

A. The President can be replaced by an acting President through action taken by himself or by others.

192. Q. How may the President ask to be replaced by an acting President?

A. The President informs the president pro tempore of the Senate and the Speaker of the House of Representatives, in writing, that he is unable to carry out the powers and duties of his office. The Vice-President then becomes Acting President.

193. Q. How long does the Vice-President remain as Acting President?

A. Until the President informs the same officers of Congress, in writing, that he is able to return and fulfill his office.

194. Q. What "others" may have the President replaced by an acting President?

A. The Vice-President and a majority of the President's Cabinet (or some other group Congress may decide upon by law) can inform the same officers of Congress, in writing, that the President is unable to fulfill his office. The Vice-President becomes Acting President if this is done.

195. Q. How does the President resume his office when he is able?

A. The President informs the same officers of Congress, in writing, that he is able to resume office. Which he does, unless, within four days, the Vice-President and a majority of the President's Cabinet (or some other group Congress may decide upon by law) inform the same officers of Congress, in writing, that the President is unable to fulfill his office.

196. Q. What happens then?

    A. Congress decides whether or not the President is capable.

197. Q. How large a vote does it take to decide that the President is incapable of fulfilling his office?
    A. A two-thirds vote of both houses.

198. Q. What if Congress is not in session?
    A. Congress must assemble within forty-eight hours.

199. Q. How long does Congress have to decide?
    A. Twenty-one days or, if not in session, twenty-one days after coming to session.

200. Q. What are some reasons the President would be unable to carry out the powers and duties of his office?
    A. A wound from an attempted assassination, prolonged physical illness, or mental disability.

201. Q. What age requirement for voting does Amendment 26 set?
    A. Eighteen years of age.

202. Q. When was each of the last sixteen amendments ratified?
    A. Amendment 11, 1798.
       Amendment 12, 1804.
       Amendment 13, 1865.
       Amendment 14, 1868.
       Amendment 15, 1870.
       Amendment 16, 1913.
       Amendment 17, 1913.
       Amendment 18, 1919.
       Amendment 19, 1920.
       Amendment 20, 1933.
       Amendment 21, 1933.
       Amendment 22, 1951.
       Amendment 23, 1961.
       Amendment 24, 1964.
       Amendment 25, 1967.
       Amendment 26, 1971.

203. Q. Where may the Constitution be seen today?
    A. The National Archives, Washington, D. C.

Answers to Check Yourself Exercises

Pages 18-19
democratic republic
indirect
central government
national government
federal government
contract
people
consent
citizen
obeyed
cooperate
Articles of Confederation
executive
judiciary
states
1781
1789
Philadelphia
revise
constitution
federal
Great Compromise
Commercial Compromise
Three-Fifths Compromise
divided
federal government
states
people
Constitution
ratified
three fourths
supreme
Federalists
Anti-Federalists
Constitution

1788
1789

Pages 32-33
Preamble
more perfect union
justice
domestic tranquillity
common defense
general welfare
liberty
ourselves
posterity
legislative
Congress
houses
House of Representatives
Senate
twenty-five
citizen
seven
district
state
two
Speaker of the House
thirty
citizen
nine
state
six
President
Vice-President
vote
tie vote
president pro tempore
population

two
impeachment
trying
trial
Chief Justice of the
   United States
impeached
expelled
two-thirds
states' legislatures
Tuesday
Monday
November
even
once
January 3
qualifications
majority
journal
Congressional Record
time
place
adjourn
three

Pages 38-39
services
60,662.50
79,125
Vice-President
office space
postage
money
treason
felony
breach of peace
congressional immunity
created
increase
salary
office

United States
tax
either
majority
majority
sign
law
veto
objections
veto
two-thirds
signs
vetoes
ten
law
signature
adjourns
ten
law
pocket veto
study
recommend
order
resolution
both
bill

Pages 45-46
taxes
money
credit
commerce
foreign
interstate
naturalization
money
value
value
money
standard
measures

counterfeiters
post offices
post
copyright
patent
courts
Supreme Court
sea
international
war
support
militias
laws
rebellions
invasion
militias
District of Columbia
federal government
powers
elastic clause
implied
habeas corpus
rebellion
invasion
attainder
ex post facto
exports
advantages
water
act of Congress
nobility
treaty
money
gold
silver
attainder
ex post facto
obligation
nobility
imports
exports

troops
states
countries
invaded
imminent

Pages 55-56
President
Vice-President
President's Cabinet
carried out
electors
electors
senators
representatives
electoral college
electoral
President of the Senate
both houses
majority
electoral
three
electoral
majority
electoral
Senate
two
electoral
Tuesday
Monday
November
four
Monday
second Wednesday
December
January 6
thirty-five
natural-born
fourteen
qualifications
Vice-President

Speaker of the House
president pro tempore of
  the Senate
Cabinet officers
created
three
created
200,000
allowances
79,125
four
two
Twenty-second
oath
swears
affirms
office
Commander in Chief
special
departments
reprieves
pardons
impeached
consent
ambassadors
consuls
Supreme Court justices
consent
temporary
state of the union
representatives
officers
treason
bribery
misdemeanors

Page 62
Supreme Court
inferior courts
Supreme Court
courts of appeals
district courts

Court of Claims
Court of Customs and
  Patent Appeals
Court of International
  Trade
Tax Court
President
consent
life
impeached
lowered
interpret
federal
state
local
original
appellate
nine
Chief
eight associate
jury
war
enemies
two witnesses
confesses
family
corruption of blood
forfeiture

Pages 69-70
laws
records
court decisions
rights
privileges
vote
extradition
divided
Congress
state's legislature
two
parts

152 THE CONSTITUTION OF THE UNITED STATES

two
legislatures
Congress
territories
properties
representative
invasion
domestic violence
two thirds
convention
two thirds
states' legislatures
three fourths
states' legislatures
conventions
three fourths
take away
equal representation
Senate
laws
state constitutions
state laws
federal
enforced
legislative
executive
judicial
support
United States Constitution
religious

Pages 78-79
religion
speech
press
assembly
petition
bear arms
militias
quarter soldiers
war

search
seizure
warrant
indicted
grand jury
double jeopardy
testify
executed
imprisoned
fined
due process
public
fair price
promptly
public
jury
charges
witnesses
witnesses
lawyer
court
twenty
jury
unreasonably
fines
cruel
unusual
torture
branding
rights
rights
states
people
exclusive
denied

Pages 92-94
federal
citizens
state
citizens

subjects	governor
foreign country	temporary appointment
President	special election
Vice-President	manufacture
number	sale
candidate	transportation
certified	intoxicating liquors
Washington, D. C.	women
President of the Senate	noon
houses	January 20
Congress	noon
majority	January 3
electoral	Vice-President-elect
three	qualify
electoral	Vice-President-elect
majority	who
electoral	selected
two	prohibition
electoral	prohibition
slavery	President
work	two terms
enabling acts	President
born	two
naturalized	one
citizen	President
state	two
rights	two
privileges	Truman
life	District of Columbia
liberty	electors
property	District of Columbia
law	electors
representatives	electors
Congress	three
proportion	poll tax
vote	removed
race	died
color	resigned
income tax	Vice-President
people	nominates
senators	vacancy

confirm

majority

president pro tempore

Speaker of the House

powers

duties

Acting President

majority

president pro tempore

Speaker of the House

powers

duties

Acting President

four

majority

decide

forty-eight hours

twenty-one days

two-thirds

eighteen